Aquarian Age Philosophy

By
EDWARD DOANE

*One of a special limited edition
this is copy number*

FOUNDATION OF SCIENTIFIC SPIRITUAL UNDERSTANDING
P. O. Box 93
Redondo Beach, California 90277, U.S.A.

Copyright, 1969

by Edward Doane

Published with the assistance of Edward Doane's co-workers, students and friends to honor his GOLDEN ANNIVERSARY with the Brotherhood of Light, these writings—never presented in book form, and some never published—were selected because of the tremendous response they brought from stellarians around the world.

Cover design by Carlos G. Rico

Printed in the United States of America by
GRAPHIC ARTS PRESS
Downey, California 90241

Remember the Hermetic Law: "As it is below, so it is above, or as on earth, so in the sky."

The Light that shines from the pinnacle of truth can never grow dim; the fogs of ignorance and superstition may obscure but cannot extinguish. It is your duty and work to aid human improvement, to put forth every effort to dispel that fog and set the bells of good tidings to ringing, peace on earth and good will to all.

T. H. Burgoyne
The Light of Egypt

TABLE OF CONTENTS

	PAGE
FOREWORD	7
FIFTY GOLDEN YEARS	9

PART I

PHILOSOPHY

EVOLUTIONARY TIDES OF A NEW AGE	15
THE DAWNING AQUARIAN AGE	19
LET THERE BE LIGHT	26
USE YOUR MIND	30
MAN VERSUS GOD	34
EXPERIENCE: THE TEACHER	39
THE DIVINE IMAGE	41
GOD AND YOU	43
HEALING PRAYER	46

PART II

PSYCHOLOGY AND ALCHEMY

PROPER PERSPECTIVE	47
CHANGE DEMANDS PROGRESS	52
EVOLVING CONSCIOUSNESS	56
SELF-MASTERY AND ATTAINMENT	57
HABITS FOR ETERNAL PLEASURE	61
MORAL CONCEPTS	67
SECURITY UNDER GOD'S LAW	68
LOVE IS NOT FOR SALE	74
THE ANCIENT ALCHEMISTS	75
AQUARIAN AGE HOROSCOPE	78

PART III

ASTROLOGY AND EXTRASENSORY PERCEPTION

ASTROLOGY: ART OR SCIENCE	79
HOW ASTROLOGY WORKS	86
ENERGY CAPTURE, STORAGE, RELEASE	92
ASTROLOGY AND HEALTH	97
EXPERIENCES	114
AQUARIAN AGE GUIDANCE	118

Astrology is the science of finding and utilizing the natural potentialities as indicated in the planetary chart at birth. It becomes a religion when it shows the individual how these natural tendencies can and should be utilized for the benefit of all mankind and the furtherance of the purposes of Deity.

Edward Doane

Foreword

THE PURPOSE OF MAN is the progression of his soul, and the anthem of the universe is eternal progression.

Man lives in an ever evolving universe. Nothing remains stationary. Change is a necessary element of creation. Resisting change leads to degeneration.

We may ask, "Are all changes good?" The test is where man comes in. He can exercise his free will to choose. Once the choice is made, man needs to accept the responsibility for that choice. To put it in other words—to pay the price.

Before an intelligent choice can be made, man needs to ask himself, "Who am I?" And because no soul is ever lost; "Where am I going?" Then as he leaves behind the material things of life, he needs to ask, "What will I take with me?"

Thoughts of old outmoded beliefs that tend to crystallize man's very existence should be discarded. Even the cells in his body must give way. A Bible reference implies the changing of one's mind: "Behold! I make all things new!"

Each Great Age left its heritage with mankind. This Age of Aquarius requires the knowledge of not accepting facts blindly, but of searching out and accepting facts that stand investigation and lead to spiritual understanding of everything in the universe.

Because science has now demonstrated that so many of the beliefs of orthodoxy are erroneous, and because in this Aquarian Age people are placing more and more reliance on science, and less and less reliance on blind belief and guessing, orthodox teachings are rapidly converting people to materialism. If materialism becomes sufficiently popular, with atomic, chemical and biological warfare available, its brutal philosophy will lead to the destruction of human life on earth.

Greater spirituality is the only thing that can save man from extinction. In this Age of Knowledge, spirituality can flourish only when people become familiar with the facts of inner-plane life as well as familiar with the facts of outer-plane life, and their relationship one to the other.

At this point on the curve of eternal progression we see the battle of materialism versus spirituality. Because of this, there is more and more a need for accurate information about things occult. Some of the significant known facts about both planes are dealt with in this book. Within these pages you will find many facets of the hermetic science explored that help to explain what makes a person tick, why he attracts the events he does, and how he can change his own destiny.

Edward Doane's ideas are like a breath of crisp, cleansing, fresh air in a plethora of books concerned with the anti-hero, negativism, the sex revolution and violence on the materialistic side, and the gory, voodoo, misleading mystic variety on the occult side.

The purpose of this book, which is written in Mr. Doane's inimitable style, is to share, to make mankind aware of its divine heritage and glorious purpose. To give glimpses of soul progression, cosmic consciousness, illumination, to challenge, to stimulate thoughts about things that will open one's awareness in scientific spiritual understanding.

As a tribute to his Golden Anniversary with the Brotherhood of Light, his co-workers, students and friends suggested a book to include some of Mr. Doane's inspirational and helpful ideas that could be passed on to the hungry souls of this new age. These writings are selected from his notes, Sunday services, lectures, articles and papers. They do not give the complete story of occult science known today, but they introduce the various topics with which man should deeply concern himself as he adjusts to the demands of this Aquarian Age.

KATALIN B. WILLIAMS
President, FOSSU

Redondo Beach, California
November, 1969

Fifty Golden Years

EDWARD DOANE'S interest in the hermetic sciences really started more than fifty years ago. A born psychic, he entered this physical life on a Nebraska farm early in the morning on October 13, 1892, at 2:58 a.m. By the time he was six years old, he was having vivid inner-plane experiences through clairaudience and clairvoyance.

Unlike most youngsters in a large family of children who enjoy playing and fighting together, he was more apt to wander off alone in the meadows and fields so that he could be by himself and look in undisturbed on the other planes of life. The flowers, trees, birds, and wild-life were his companions. He learned to enter their consciousnesses and commune with them.

As a youth, he chafed against the strict orthodoxy of his environment. As he grew older he questioned the clergymen of the time. He did not know where else to turn to quench his insatiable curiosity about life. His questions were never answered to his satisfaction.

An inveterate reader, he had read from cover to cover the dictionary, the Bible, the Encyclopedia Britanica and other tomes. Having a photographic mind and a retentive memory, all of this information remained with him into adulthood. Later, his friends were to dub him a "walking encyclopedia" or the "professor," which inadvertently goes along with Virgo rising in his horoscope.

His deep reflected thought and concentrated meditation eventually lead to his forming an independent philosophy of his own while still young. It would be many years though before he would meet anyone who could "talk his language."

With his natural love of nature, growing and living things, he chose to attend the College of Agriculture at the University of Nebraska after he left high school. There he conducted fascinating experiments and studied animals, growing things, breeding, seeds, and the natural sciences. Always an active person, during these years he hardly slept at all. He worked nights to put himself through college and also worked in the vacation seasons.

Wide experience through these years and after gave him the insight to understand the viewpoints on all levels of life. This helped him in his later work as a minister. Eventually he was to become a tugboat captain, a commercial fisherman, a horse wrangler, a lumberjack, a fish and game warden, a cook, a realtor, an insurance agent, and an interior decorator (which satisfied his Libra potentials, as his work took him into some of the finest estates in the country).

When World War I came along, he was called up with the other boys of his age. His organizational and leadership ability were detected immediately. He received a quick promotion and was placed in charge of ordinance.

Shortly after being discharged from the army, he was residing in the south when the 1918 influenza epidemic hit hard. Being the kind of man he is, he got out of his own bed and helped the short-handed nurses and doctors attend the other patients, while having a temperature of 104° himself. From this experience, and later through his friendships with pharmacists and doctors, his interest in preventing illness was stimulated. His agile mind sought for ways that would help to keep people from becoming ill.

Finally, in 1919, he met a group of people who, to his pleasant surprise, spoke in the same philosophical terms he had adopted years before. This personal thrill came to him when he attended a Brotherhood of Light meeting in Tampa, Florida. In a flash, he knew he had "come home," as it were.

From then until the present day, he has worked for this Great Cause. During this meeting, he realized that his earlier inner-plane experiences had been with the Brothers of Light and that they had been guiding him through the necessary experiences that his soul needed to fit it for its cosmic work.

His sensitive and probing mind, as well as his argument against the *status quo,* had fired his constant search for truth. Now, at long last after all these years, he knew in his heart he had found his truth in the Religion of the Stars. It follows that with Mercury being his Dominant Planet he got right down to work. He studied morning, noon and night. He would fall on the bed exhausted fully dressed. Like Henry Ford, he slept in short intervals, waking refreshed to go on with his studies. It was not too long before an inner-plane Brother came to him and guided his efforts.

Never one to dabble with anything, he had to prove or disprove for himself all of the theories presented in the Brotherhood of Light Lessons. This eventually led him to specialize in three important fields: psychic phenomena, astronomy and stellar healing. His findings have been published through the years in many occult, scientific and astrological magazines.

After this extensive period of study, he began to teach classes in

Florida, and then widened his scope by lecturing state-wide. His efforts came to the attention of Elbert Benjamine, Founder of the Church of Light. Thus began a long, intimate, harmonious relationship which had a deep impact upon the material presented in the Brotherhood of Light Courses, by C. C. Zain (pen-name of Elbert Benjamine). Soon after, under the influence of the inner-plane Brothers, Mr. Doane moved to Miami, and in 1935 established the Miami Church of Light.

One special area of his occult research was psychic in nature. For a number of years, he conducted a group of B. of L. students, who had passed ten or more degrees or initiation in the work, on inner-plane excursions. They practiced astral travel and extension of consciousness. To their enlightenment, they visited temples, libraries and other places of learning and saw wonders that would be difficult to describe in physical words, such as four-dimensional horoscopes.

These investigations and the results of the trials and errors made to contact the astral plane formed the basis of knowledge which eventually led Elbert Benjamine (C. C. Zain), author or the Brotherhood of Light Lessons, to change the content of the Lessons as well as the Not Sold Manuscripts awarded to initiates.

The shift of emphasis was mainly from the negative, mediumistic Piscean Age concept of approaching and producing psychic phenomena to the Aquarian Age safe approach of positive, intellectual, extrasensory perception. The latter advocates an extension of consciousness allowing the traveler to keep in control at all times, thus protecting himself from the dangers lurking on its lower realms.

Doane also managed to arrest the attention of some scientists who constantly mouthed without analysis what they had been told—astrology is a *pseudo-science.* During the 1930's, he had been studying all of the sciences, and he chose to challenge astronomers.

He felt it was necessary to educate scientists to the fact that there was more to astrology than the "entertainment" variety. In the exchange of voluminous correspondence covering a period of five years, he posed ten questions on the very forces that astronomers and physicists used in their work.

His summary of their responses was presented in a well-received paper, entitled "A Critical Analysis of the Fallacies in Astronomy," at a convention of the American Federation of Scientific Astrologers (now the American Federation of Astrologers).

During this period, some of the astronomers wrote him saying they would have to agree with his theories, but that their private opinions were not for publication. In those days the atmosphere was entirely different than it is today. It is no disgrace for an academician to talk about astrology and such in 1970. But in the 1930's! It meant exile or something worse.

Another area in which Doane actively researched was health and healing. Many of his conclusions are now embraced in Zain's "Stellar Healing" and "Personal Alchemy." Due to his natural psychic ability, he was a natural healer.

He employed stellar healing, which is an individualized approach to a person's problems. It is conducted in such a manner that the patient's natal chart with its progressions act as a guide to select the energies and colors of the planets indicating the trouble. Then the antidote rays are employed to neutralize or transmute the discord.

Laying on of the hands was another of his effective specialties until his later work forced him to live a life more involved with the material aspects of spreading the Religion of The Stars. He also emphasized diet—both mental and physical—and championed juice therapy (for sources of vitamins and minerals) long before it was fashionable to have a juicer or blender.

His articles on astrology and health brought an avalanche of mail. They also put him in touch with medical doctors, osteopaths, naturopaths, absent healers, dieticians and others interested in health. He gained a tremendous amount of information from these various sources. In his successful treatments, he added the techniques of mental and spiritual alchemy and applied all with the guidance of the personal horoscope.

Working with this subject, his active psychic senses brought through many revealing factors about the physical body. During the healing period, he clairvoyantly viewed the organ affected and described the character of the disease manifesting according to the natal chart of the patient. Due to this sensitiveness, about 20 years before doctors recognized it, he said that the bone marrow was the birth place of the blood cells. As you read the cases cited in this book, you will understand his approach to psychic diagnosis.

In the 1930's, he wrote the Church of Light healing service, and he became the first minister to hold weekly healing services with the assistance of the Brothers on the inner planes. These healing periods were open to the public as well as to those who wished absent treatment. Many were helped through the years as his record of case histories demonstrates. After moving to Los Angeles, he continued this weekly service. Then he and his wife, Doris Chase Doane, started a daily healing ministry on April 18, 1959, which they still conduct at noon Pacific Time.

Even though Elbert Benjamine and Edward Doane had had many contacts by mail and on the astral plane, it was not until 1938 that they met face to face. With Fred Skinner, co-founder and then Vice President of The Church of Light, they met on the West Coast to discuss the future activities of the work. As a result of this conference, Mr. Doane was placed in charge of all Church of Light activities on the East Coast.

He had been ordained as a minister in 1934, in Miami, Florida, where he kept the doors of the Church open to the public seven days a week—a record never matched by any other center.

People from all welks of life came to him for help. He always encouraged them to study and learn to apply the Religion of The Stars to their own problems. In his lectures, he gave substance and reality to the ideals presented in the textbooks. In the early days when astrology and occultism were not as widely accepted as they are today, scoffers and skeptics would come to a meeting hoping to sneer and make snide remarks. They stayed to admire.

His dignity, humility, sincerity and honesty commands the high esteem and respect of thousands of students and co-workers around the world. The late Elbert Benjamine said of him, "Ed would bend over backwards to be fair and honest, and that is shown by his Best Planet, Saturn, located in the first house of his horoscope."

Mr. Doane was the first minister in C. of L. history to hold weekly Sunday morning services. When he later went to Los Angeles, he started them there as well. At one of these services in Florida, during the middle of his lecture, a vision kept thrusting itself up before his attention insistently. He had to work hard to keep above it in order to continue with his talk. The vision was one of blood, soot and smoke streaming across the American Flag. It was all he could manage to complete the service. Immediately afterwards, the news came that the Japanese had attacked Pearl Harbor at the hour of his insistent vision.

By the late 30's he was active in the program to standardize astrology. All of the larger occult and astrology schools at that time engaged in this effort. He was also one of the first Board Members of the American Federation of Astrologers, serving that organization as third vice president.

In October of 1943, Mr. Benjamine called him to Los Angeles to serve as Vice President of The Church of Light. He moved west and took charge of the Mail Order Department. Soon after, he married Doris Chase Doane. Then he, Mrs. Doane and Mr. Benjamine worked closely through the years spreading the teachings.

With the demise of Elbert Benjamine in November, 1951, at Mr. Benjamine's request, Edward Doane became President of the Church. All through his administration, he gained much cooperation. His understanding of people, analytical brilliance and creative thinking, as he applied the spiritual teachings, allowed him to carry on his cosmic work in harmony. His best weapon against discord was the personal example he set for others.

He lives and practices to the letter the tenets of the Brotherhood of Light. In this manner he has always brought out the best in people. A shining example of a person who is at once simple, human and courageous. Having an instinct for the rightness of things, he built the organization so that it won converts in almost every country on the face of the globe.

While directing Church affairs, he was responsible for accumulating $50,000 donations for the Building Fund. The larger donations were given due to the donor's personal love of him and of his work. His overriding commitment as a leader was to fairness. He always took the theme of all souls being independent, working out their cosmic destinies. He stressed that their freedom was important in the Divine Plan.

When he retired as President of the Church, the Board of Directors expressed their gratitude for his long years of service and gave him a weekly pension and a place to live for the rest of his life.

Yes, years ago Edward Doane was a pioneer with a dream—not in the sense of the early explorer or railroad men who worked on land. Doane worked on hearts. His dream was woven of mental stuff—the practice of mental and spiritual alchemy, to which he devoted his life, telling others how to go about making this transmutation so that they could relish the elixer of life both here and hereafter.

His 50 Golden Years of dedicated service to spiritual work have made it possible for students to progress along the pathway . . . and they will continue to do so long after he has taken up his work on the next plane.

A Tribute

We salute you, Edward Doane, on Your Golden Anniversary. May you remain with us physically, as long as possible, to give us the benefit of your understanding, the inspiration of your kindliness, the example of how to transmit the Brotherhood of Light vibrations, and inspire others to do so. We can only hope to be able to present an example as successfully, as faithfully, and at the vibratory level of your efforts.

Congratulations, good wishes, and deep appreciation.

YOUR STUDENTS

Philosophy

EVOLUTIONARY TIDES OF A NEW AGE

I. ENLIGHTENED humanity in the Aquarian Age is faced with the great task of building here on earth a truly enlightened and humanitarian civilization. This demands that all people of the earth have Freedom of Worship, Freedom of Expression, Freedom from Fear, Freedom from Want, and that all men and women of Good Will adopt as the constant and dominating motive of their lives the idea that they should *Contribute Their Utmost to Universal Welfare.*

Freedom of information is essential to true freedom of any sort. Therefore, in order to understand and develop the potentials of their own souls and to understand their relationship to God and all other life forms, mankind should be familiar with the Facts of Astrology, the Facts of Extra Sensory Perception, the Facts of Induced Emotion and the Facts of Directed Thinking.

The most important thing in all of Cosmos is God's Great Plan of Progressive Evolution. To the individual, the most important thing of all is the progress of his own soul.

Personal progress requires effort on the part of each to learn the facts about his soul and how he may gain the higher states of consciousness that lead to ultimate conscious cooperation with God. To supply the information essential to such understanding and progress to make it accessible to all, the Brotherhood of Light Lessons were written.

The last half century has brought more technological progress than the preceding two thousand years embracing the Piscean Age with its keyphrase of I Believe. In the Aquarian Age, whose keyphrase is I Know, the impact of high tension energies from the inner planes upon the subconscious mental organisms (souls) of mankind has brought restlessness and inventiveness and the desire to know and progress to a peak greater than little earth has known in all its recorded history.

Great as the difference is between the box kite planes of Kitty Hawk and the supersonic jets of today, what has occurred is but the feeble beginnings of potential accomplishment.

However apparently great the progress of technology may seem at the present time, by far the greatest achievement along this line during the present age will be the mechanical (electronic) contact with the inner planes of life. This contact will lead to the death of materialism and dispel erroneous religious ideas of the soul and life hereafter.

Freedom loving Uranus, ruler of Aquarius, equals the individualistic urge in the subconscious mind. As a natural consequence of the dawning of the Aquarian Age, a great desire for freedom is sweeping the earth. In the national sense it manifests as the emergence of new nations. In the personal sense it expresses as the great surge for equality under the law both in the United States and elsewhere. This surge for individual freedom and national freedom will not subside and in due time will embrace all nations and all peoples.

Accomplishing the Aquarian Age purpose of building a truly humanitarian and enlightened civilization here on earth necessitates many changes. One is the establishment of representative forms of government in all of the countries of the earth. The attainment of the desired freedoms is impossible under any other form.

The United States offers one of the best possible examples of representative government. It is only under such a governmental form that it is possible to obtain the essential Freedoms of Worship and Expression - the essential freedom of information.

Finding means of abolishing war as a method of settling differences between nations is imperative. This requires the establishment of a united nations organization and the disarmament of all the nations of the earth, except for the forces necessary to keep order within the individual nations. It also requires a United Nations Force to prevent any nation from starting an aggressive war against another nation and an adequate Intelligence Force to make sure that no nation secretly builds armaments to try to take over the world.

The present United Nations must undergo considerable reorganization if it is to serve the purpose.

Vast evolutionary changes are essential within the nations behind the Iron Curtain as well as within some of those in the so-called free world before it will be done, but the creation of a world-wide public opinion for the abolition of war and the building of a greater **degree of peace** on earth is necessary.

Unilateral disarmament in the present world conditions is an open invitation to disaster and slavery. Atheistic materialism, through the force of arms if possible, is determined to dominate the earth. If not through force of arms, they will try to achieve their goal through destruction of freedom of information and freedom of expression.

These forces, motivated as they are by the principalities of Darkness not of this earth, are exceedingly clever at misrepresentation, distortion of facts, and suppression of information favorable to astrology, extrasensory perception, and the evidence that the personality survives physical death.

The Legions of Light on the inner plane are equally determined that God's Plan for the New Civilization shall be realized and that a spiritually enlightened humanitarian civilization shall be built on earth.

In academic institutions, the tools of the principalities of Darkness often creep in to convince the students: That death ends everything as far as the individual soul is concerned. That man does not have a soul. That there is nothing at all to extrasensory perception or astrology. Quite often these dupes of the Dark Forces are completely unaware that they are being used to keep mankind chained to the brute level of expression.

In almost all religious organizations and outside of any formalized religious organization are men and women whose spiritual desires and motives are such that their minds can be easily reached by members of the Legions of Light on the inner planes. They can be impressed to take such stands and such actions as will ultimately lead to the effective building of the required (by God's Plan) new humanitarian civilization on earth.

As the Spirit we call God permeates and actively directs all of Cosmos, it is impossible for one person or one group to have a monopoly on the ways and means of acquiring spirituality or information as to the essential steps leading to the fulfillment of the Divine Plan for this Aquarian Age.

Our attitude: The new civilization must be built on earth. It is not so important who does the building. It is of paramount importance that the building be done.

In the years just ahead, the evolutionary processes required to bring about the changes will be markedly stepped up. From January 21 to March 12, 1962 Aquarius received a lot of stimulation. Most of the attention was centered on the Solar Eclipse of February 4, 1962 and some were sure that it was of dire portent.[1]

Few stopped to think that God had need of a crop of human souls on earth, souls with the types of potentials mapped by the charts of those born under the periods mentioned above, in order that His Plan for the Aquarian Age might be brought into being.

In the twenty odd years just ahead these Aquarian Dominant folk will be graduating from school and entering the political life of the nations of the world. They will demand knowledge as a natural birthright. Many of them will be natural orators and thus be able to influence public opinion to a marked extent. Authoritarianism in religion or science will be rejected as a matter of course.

[1] Written in 1963

Both Uranus and Pluto are now in Virgo. With each Virgo New Moon, up to six of the ten equivalents (planets including Sun and Moon) of the basic urges of the subconscious mind will be in evidence in the charts of those born during these periods. This indicates a crop of souls who will be capable of analysis of an exceptionally high order. They will be capable of developing the information of the times (scientific and otherwise) into an understandable whole. These souls will fit into the pattern of human evolution, performing tasks that are impossible to others with different types of potential.[1]

But whatever the configurations in the sky, the birth chart of each human soul represents a valuable potential in the Divine Plan of Progressive Evolution. And whether here or hereafter, each soul will ultimately fit in to the Cosmic Whole as an intelligent cooperating part, performing the functions for which it was brought into being.

The first step an individual must take in order to make any real spiritual progress is to realize that it is impossible for any one or thing other than himself to think, feel and act for him. Then he must realize that if his responses to internal and external stimuli are discordant, thus making for unhappiness, it is up to him to make constructive changes in his habit-systems of thinking, feeling and acting.

The astrological birth-chart is the basic map of the subconscious mind. Whatever alters the subconscious mind, thus changing the character as mapped in the chart, is the result of conditioning energy. There are three factors which influence conditioning energy: (1) Progressions, indicating astrological energies on the inner plane; (2) thoughts of others and character vibrations; and by far the most important factor in conditioning responses is (3) one's own thoughts and feelings.

Thus a person's intellectual and spiritual progress is markedly speeded when he learns to apply the information obtained through the teachings of The Religion of The Stars to the problem of daily living and uses the Facts of Induced Emotion and Directed Thinking in his effort to gain usefulness, happiness and spirituality.

Analyzing an individual's psychological makeup should properly begin at the foundation as mapped by his birth chart. Because academic psychology has neglected that foundation, thus neglecting the only possible effective means of individual application of psychology, it remains to this day a hodgepodge filled with ill-defined or undefined terms which have little if any practical meaning. In time during this new age, astrology will be taught in the very academic institutions where professors of psychology now attempt to deride this Golden Key to the human mind.

One of the Spiritual Texts of Astrology containing the Golden rule states: Think and do unto others as you would have others think and do unto you. Spiritual progress demands the adoption of this concept. At the

[1] Written in 1963

present time most of the human race still functions on or near the brute level of expression. At this level little of the meaning of the above quoted text has entered the consciousness. As a consequence, little if any concern for others is evidenced.

Just what the Divine Plan of Progressive Evolution is and how it operates is unperceived and uncomprehended by most people. Therefore to demonstrate the new civilization, ways and means must be found to reach and influence millions of as yet untouched minds to make them aware of the principles and teachings of The Religion of The Stars.

The more people who study and practice our religion, the more power will be given to the thoughts broadcast from both inner and outer planes by The Legions of Light and the easier it will be for others, not of our religion but of good will and purpose, to receive inspiration and guidance as to the ways and means of building peace on earth. Peace is the harmonious relationships between peoples, as individuals, as groups and as nations.

As the evolutionary tides of the New Age grow stronger with the passage of each day, there is a tremendous task ahead in building a civilization in which peace on earth is possible. Each one of us can help in some manner to gain this desirable end. Each should start within the confines of his own soul. It is the instrument in which character must be built and which each must use to attain his highest potentiality. For as the individual character is improved, the manner in which he thinks, feels and acts toward others also changes for the better.

When all the peoples of the earth, including the leaders of nations and religions, start to thinking and doing unto others as they would have others think and do unto them, peace on earth and good will toward all mankind shall reign supreme. It is the goal toward which we must ever strive no matter how rough the way or unlikely its attainment may seem.

For this Great Work we need an understanding faith, undaunted courage and enduring patience. These we can gain as we work in Eternal Life, both here and hereafter, reaching for an ever higher degree of understanding and ability that we may better assist the Divine Plan of Progressive Evolution.

THE DAWNING AQUARIAN AGE

TO ATTAIN and maintain a high level of civilization depends upon the ability of that civilization to produce men and women of exceptional ability and power, who are willing to work with unflagging zeal for universal good. Such men and women must learn to overcome the temptation that is ever present, to sink back to the gutter of self-centeredness and use their abilities to exploit those of less intelligence and less power.

Any lack of effort on the part of the individual to keep himself on a spiritual level is immediately followed by a sinking back to the brute level in which concern is felt only for self and immediate family and friends.

It is only through the happy combination of an exceptional and unselfish leader with a people capable of putting aside less worthy desires to cooperate for the common good, that a high level of civilization can be maintained. Because a culture following the precepts of The Religion of The Stars, in which the highest devotion consists in contributing the utmost to universal welfare, is the most lofty and most satisfactory of all, it is for that very reason the most difficult to retain.

A noteworthy example is the story of the rise and fall of the Mayan Civilization, a period during which Itzamna the Initiate did so much to inculcate the teachings of The Religion of The Stars and make possible the rise of a high civilization. The ultimate destruction of the records of this civilization under the leadership of degenerate priests is a matter of record. But the conditions which made possible such destruction was the thrusting aside, by the soldiers of Kukolcan, of the One God of The Religion of The Stars and the high teachings of Itzamna and the substitution of the vicious rites and gruesome practices of Toltec religion. Thus we find the oft repeated evidence of a nation rising to a noble culture only to sink back into barbarism again becoming part of history. The process by which this degeneration follows the high cultural level is neither obscure nor strange.

Maintaining a high cultural standard requires that people be educated. This in turn demands the freedom to obtain information as to the facts of life, freedom of religion, the right to obtain freedom from want and the freedom of fear of suppression.

Throughout history, those who sought to enslave humankind have always sought to suppress information and to force the populace to conform to some pattern of thought and action. These efforts at suppression led to the destruction of the Alexandrian Library, the burning of a vast accumulation of Mayan information in the form of books and in a more modern day, the efforts of Hitler to destroy everything contrary to his insane method of thinking and the efforts of past and present leaders of Soviet Russia to suppress everything contrary to the concepts of atheistic materialism.

It matters not whether the efforts to force conformity of thought, feeling and action arise from a fanatical priesthood, as was the case during the Inquisition, or from political zealots afflicted with so much egomania that they imagine they alone are capable of determining what is best for a people or a nation; the end result of such activity has always been the destruction and fall of a civilization and the rise of a species of barbarism.

We are not the advocate or sponsor of any political party. On the contrary we are convinced that the devotees of our religion and the devotees of other religions are quite intelligent enough and quite capable enough to determine for themselves the individuals and issues they should support with their vote.

We are further convinced that great danger to the present civilization lies in the current effort to distort and withold information from the populace and in efforts to sow the dragons' teeth of racial and religious prejudice in order to attain political power.

The devotees of The Religion of The Stars will find abundant opportunity in the present environmental conditions to work for Universal Welfare through trying to teach, practice and disseminate The Religion of The Stars, thus exerting a beneficent influence upon the evolution of the present civilization toward an ever higher spiritual level.

The opportunities to gain an education through public schools need maintenance and expansion. The opportunities to gain a spiritual education by gaining a higher level of religious and intellectual freedom need to be expanded greatly through a wider freedom of information. It is only through greater freedom that the efforts of materialistic atheism to enslave mankind can be overcome and an ever more spiritually enlightened civilization be maintained.

Any slackening of effort on the part of the more enlightened of the present day can have only one inevitable result, a result so often recorded in the historical past.

The progress of an individual soul and the progress of a civilization each depend upon unselfish, intelligent effort. This effort cannot in either instance embrace hatred, fear, prejudice or anger and at the same time be an enlightened spiritual effort.

It does not require fear, hatred nor anger to build a dam in order to protect against possible floods. On the contrary, to build a good dam dispassionate planning and calm deliberate work is required. So it is with civilization; to prevent the flooding of the earth with the doctrines of materialistic atheism or the equally destructive doctrines of racial and religious prejudice, we must build a dam of spiritual enlightenment in the souls of the populace. This requires much deliberate work.

Freedom cannot be attained or maintained by adopting the methods of those who have, from time immemorial, used those methods to destroy civilizations. Through a study of the events and conditions of the past, we can realize what must be done in the present in order to build a better civilization for the future.

The world needs the happy combination of a spiritually enlightened leadership with a people who are willing to understand and work for Universal Welfare.

Even though it were possible, we of The Church of Light would not suppress any other religion no matter how much we might disagree with its teachings. This is because freedom can never be gained through suppression. The only possible way an individual or nation can have freedom is through having the right to choose for self, after an examination of available information.

We live in an age in which the struggle for dominance by the forces of darkness, represented by the actual and would-be suppressors on one side, and the forces of light, represented by those who stand for spiritual enlightenment and the utmost freedom on the other, as at its peak. In the long run it is inevitable that the forces of light will win, but the amount of suffering that will be brought to mankind before the victory of freedom and high purpose is attained depends to a very large degree on the amount of unselfish effort we are willing to spend.

The greatest civilizations are made up of individuals. The whole is the product of the many. Therefore the effort that any single individual exerts does, to some degree, determine the progress of the whole.

In the highest of past civilizations the leadership and teachings of those who embraced, in whole or in part, the principles and teachings of The Religion of The Stars has been the greatest contributing factor in the attainment of those civilizations, for to these exalted souls the populace looked for enlightenment and direction. Without exception, the gain to positions of leadership of those who rejected these principles and teachings has marked the beginning of the fall of those civilizations.

Just here, before we are accused of claiming to be the sole and only possessors of truth and high principle, let us state that the principles of, and the teachings embodied in, The Religion of The Stars are Universal property. Further, the devotees of any religion or the devotee of no religion, moved by love of God's Creation and the desire to render unselfish service, places himself in tune with the source of these teachings and may on his own see the correct pathway. No person or group in God's Great Plan of Eternal Progression is granted a monopoly in spiritual enlightenment or the right to contribute their utmost to universal welfare.

Because in the present age the means of conveying ideas has been developed to the highest point of any time in either the historical or traditional past, the communication of these ideas takes much less time and effort than ever before. It is precisely because of the high development of printing, transportation and various telecommunications that the present Aquarian Age offers the greatest opportunity to mankind to build a very high degree of truly humanitarian civilization. And it is because of this potential that those spiritual custodians of The Religion of The Stars resident on the inner planes induced C. C. Zain to place a complete exposition of our religion in writing, in the form of The Brotherhood of Light

Lessons, so that mankind might have as easy access as possible to the principles and teachings which allow the highest degree of culture to be attained on earth.

It is also because the means of conveying ideas, having become easier in the present than at any time in the past, affords an equal opportunity to convey distortion and falsehood and attempts to stir up racial and religious strife that the responsibility for positive thought and action is so great upon the part of those of us who perceive the desires of Deity relative to evolving a truly humanitarian civilization upon earth during the present age. We must not, therefore, hesitate to sow the seeds of spiritual enlightenment in order to reap the harvest of a continually evolving civilization, thus assisting in the fulfillment of the Divine Plan.

The field of potential effort is without limit. What is needed most during this period of struggle and transition is a populace willing to cooperate for the ultimate benefit of all, and enlightened leaders willing to try to discern and follow the Divine Plan.

Each individual who perceives the necessity for effort in order to assist the evolution of the whole of civilization can assist through doing his or her utmost to help spread The Religion of The Stars. To practice and teach, inspiring others to obtain the intellectual and spiritual growth that follows such practice and teaching, is one of the best methods. Helping others to carry on the work through financial assistance is still another good method.

It is a Hermetic Axiom that the individual soul can receive light only as it gives light and it can give light only as it receives light. So also can any particular civilization and culture as achieved by any nation inspire other peoples of a different sort of civilization and culture to adopt its principles, teachings and practices only as it serves as an example of having received light that markedly benefits its people and is thus capable of giving to others something infinitely better than that which they have.

There is no substitute for practicing what is preached. The abandonment of democratic practices and principles at home in order to try to combat the tyranny that threatens from abroad is to become tyrants and fall heir to the very principles and practices that have so successfully destroyed the cultures and civilizations of the past. And it is the surest method of advertising to the world that our vaunted culture is only a sham of pretense; for what people would desire to throw off one set of tyrants only to become slaves of another set of tyrants who, like the first set, were determined to practice suppression of ideas and allow only the conformity of opinion that they already possess.

We can cultivate a desire for our form of civilization and our culture only as we demonstrate to the rest of the world that it allows the greatest degree of freedom of thought, freedom of-expression and freedom of religion to be found anywhere on earth. Naturally we must protect, with force of arms if need be, our various countries in the free world. We must also take such measures as are necessary to protect against sabotage and subversion within each country. But unless we are willing to follow the course of the fallen civilizations of the past, we must maintain the greatest possible degree of freedom within.

This world of ours is at the turning point. We are either going ahead to the attainment and maintenance of an ever higher degree of civilization through a continually greater degree of freedom, or we are going to again learn from history that we have learned nothing from history, falling, through adopting the methods and practices of tyrants, into a temporary form of a dark age.

Fanaticism, whether of the political variety or the practice of a zealot under the banner of some religion, always seeks to destroy freedom through suppression of ideas and the attempted forcing of conformity. Ever and always, the bait of combatting something not in conformity with the welfare of a culture and civilization is held out, to serve as an excuse for the destructive excesses that have ever led to the downfall of cultures and civilizations of the past.

The attempted substitution of guilt by association for the time-proven practice of guilt by positive proof was the method followed during the Inquisition. It is also the method followed by Hitler and his cohorts as well as the method followed by the Soviet.

It is quite as unfair as accusing a rabbit, grazing in the midst of a herd of sheep, of being a sheep, and then proceeding to try to make mutton of him by butchery. Or trying to persecute the sheep for association with the rabbit who, after all, was eating some grass that might have made good mutton had the sheep been sufficiently alert to this subversion to chase the innocent rabbit off the range.

There is no form of subversion greater than that which seeks to destroy the free exchange of ideas concerned with obtaining the highest degree of intellectual and spiritual progress. Regardless of political or religious stature, whosoever seeks to suppress such freedoms is quite as dangerous a subversive as any avowed communist or fascist, for whether he realizes it or not he is working to destroy the culture and the civilization of the free world. He is using the very tactics and advocating the very principles that have in the past caused the downfall of the greatest civilizations achieved up to a particular time.

Freedom is very much the business of the devotees of The Religion of The Stars to best promote the continued rise of our civilization and prevent its downfall, we must ever strive to expand and extend the freedoms we have cherished and where necessary take whatever means are needed to prevent their destruction by any form of tyranny, whether it arises from without or within the various countries of the free world.

If we are to serve as an example to the peoples of the countries already under some form of tyranny, we must continually strive to expand and extend these freedoms that they may be inspired to throw off their enslaving chains; that they may do away with iron and other curtains preventing the free flow of ideas between all the peoples of the earth, ideas bringing understanding and desire to practice the principles and teachings that in the past have led to the highest cultures man has known. And that they may be inspired to build for themselves cultures and civilizations in which freed souls are able to know and enjoy boundless opportunity for intellectual and spiritual progress as well as the physical fruits of an advanced humanitarian Aquarian Age.

The great initiates of the past have never turned aside from a task because great obstacles were in the way of its fulfillment. On the contrary, when the task was accepted as a work to be done it was regarded as a challenge to be met, and in accordance with the teachings of The Religion of The Stars the pleasure technique was used in finding the ways and means of doing the necessary work. These great souls were ever satisfied with doing the very best they could, in cooperation with The Legions of Light on the inner planes, to see that the work was carried through to the best possible conclusion.

Never has any true Initiate or The Legions of Light condoned or used the tactics that have led to the destruction of cultures through the attempted suppression of the freedoms, so necessary to the progress of a great civilization. Neither have these Initiates adopted a peace at any price attitude which could lead only to slavery.

Everyone can do something. It is because of this fact that throughout The Religion of The Stars there is not one single "thou shalt not." On the contrary, positive thinking, feeling and action is taught and it is advocated that one become so occupied with doing something to assist the progress of individuals and whole civilizations that there is no time left to indulge in soul-destroying negativism.

Souls make progress by doing and civilizations are built by doers. It is the practice of positive thinking that leads us to alter the old saying, "Watchman, what of the night?" and substitute "Worker, what of the day?"

In this world of ours, boundless opportunities are present for each of us in accordance with present talents and abilities, to contribute to Universal Welfare. What is much better is the fact that there are also boundless opportunities for each of us to gain new abilities and continually expand these abilities to enjoy our God-given right to freedom of the soul and work in the evolvement of a still higher and better civilization. In this dawning Aquarian Age, the highest civilization ever attained on earth is possible to mankind. Whether that becomes a reality depends upon the efforts of each and every one of us.

LET THERE BE LIGHT

TEN THOUSAND years from now, perhaps scientists, digging in the ruins of the present civilization, will speculate about the types of people inhabiting those ancient areas under consideration. They will likely search for written records and try to decipher strange languages in order to understand the thoughts, religions and the governments of those ancient races.

Civilizations evolve and decline. Mountain ranges thrust up and then—through the slow process of erosion—become level plains. Continents rise and sink below the waves. Evolutionary life processes of the earth and its habitant forms advances through the ages, as God's Great Plan of Progression unfolds in Ageless Eternity.

Periodic destruction of large portions of civilization by fire (extreme volcanic action) and by water (floods) occur time and time again. Life forms appear and vanish from the earth as the great process of evolution continues. The new continuously arises to displace the old.

Established governments flourish for a time and then change to meet new conditions imposed by evolutionary environment, or die as outmoded forms if successful adaptation is not accomplished.

Religions appear, live for a time and vanish through degeneration. They become so modified that their originators would never recognize them, finally vanishing from view in the great structural changes imposed upon earth by the Great Plan of Eternal Progression. Man is prone to view these vast changes as terrible tragedies, because so many of his particular kind of life are eradicated from the earth. The visual scope—common to mankind—is limited by a self-centered viewpoint, preventing the comprehension of the methods used by Eternal God to insure that the course of evolution proceed exactly according to Plan.

Man undergoes earthly schooling to develop intelligence and understanding. Sufficient development enables each individual to begin to fulfill a destiny for which he was called into being. Humankind establishes governments, religions, social patterns, moral codes, etc., endeavoring to satisfy its inherent basic urges. The hereditary Drive for Significance or Power Urge (astrologically, the Sun) serves an evolutionary purpose of keeping life forms struggling for importance. When this urge is perverted as Rule or Ruin, the desire to dictate is inherent.

Perverted power urges have moved religious leaders to forbid the study of physics, and the relief of pain. They ruled that those who disobeyed would be jailed, tortured and slain—all in the name of a merciful God. The desire to dictate has caused scientists to try to suppress psychic investigation, and to ridicule (without study) astrology. They attempt to promote the false idea that every existing thing can be explained by an examination of the purely physical.

This desire to dictate led—in its extreme—to the dialectical materialism of Communism and is, to this day, aided and abetted by the blind materialist. So self-hypnotized by his false sense of importance, nothing can be real to the materialist that he cannot weigh and measure on already existing devices.

Even to this day some religious leaders try to promulgate the idea that nothing can be good or true that does not originate in their particular creed. They appear to believe that honest investigation of inner-plane facts of the human soul or outer-plane facts of astrology and its esoteric significance is certainly to be condemned to eternal hell fire.

Yet if one questions—steering clear of mental associations which cause biased emotional reactions—these pundits as to whether they believe in freedom of religion and freedom of thought and expression, they will most stoutly affirm that they do. Because these would-be dictators can no longer do away with the opposition by jailing, torturing and slaying, they resort to the next step. They take legislative steps, no matter how perverted, to try to destroy the freedoms of those with opposing views. Naturally, such activity would ultimately lead (if successful) to another dark age and the total destruction of the very freedoms in which they claim to believe.

We do not need to speculate as to what happens to freedom of religion and freedom of expression under the Hitlers, the Mussolinis, the Stalins, or the religious leaders of the various Inquisitions. That is history.

We are very positive that representative government must allow the greatest freedom of worship and freedom of expression. We are equally positive that any person or group of persons who labor to destroy for others—under any pretext whatsoever—the freedoms claimed for self are actually trying to undermine the institution of Freedom and establish dictatorship through forcing conformity to their own narrow opinions.

To assist God's Great Plan of Progressive Evolution, it is necessary to understand something of the realities of life and evolution. It is necessary to realize that the Great God has a Plan that is being and will be fulfilled. C. C. Zain in the "Evolution of Life" has this to say: "It is not surprising that man in the past had erroneous ideas about himself, about the earth and about life after physical dissolution. Nor at the present day do we possess all important information on these subjects. It is not to criticize the ignorance of the past or that of the present, that these matters are being mentioned. It is to point out how the iron curtain of fear erected by orthodoxy has impeded investigation and has made people afraid to recognize facts which are essential to their present and future well being. And to emphasize that this iron curtain of fear erected by orthodoxy must be lifted if man is to live to best advantage."

Man must learn to accept full responsibility for his own thoughts, feelings and actions. The soul refusing to face the facts of life, regardless of some erroneous teaching, prefers to remain a slave to error rather than to enjoy the freedom resulting only from a free-will acceptance of responsibility and a free-will uniting of the soul to God's Great Plan. Man must take up his individual burden and walk in the Light!

Individual changes come about when habit systems of reaction to the forces (including those astrological) of environment are changed. The greater the amount of self-centeredness that prevails, the more painful experiences are attracted. The greater the degree of spiritual understanding one has, the more happiness one finds in life.

Natural upheavals effectively destroy areas of existing civilizations, bringing great changes and a complete new set of environmental conditions. As a consequence, the remaining life must devise ways and means of survival. Tragic as this may seem, considered solely from a limited physical viewpoint, it is absolutely essential in order that workers of specific types in the Divine Plan be evolved. Let us never forget that the idea of an All-wise God carries with it the idea of a smooth-working plan of evolution—a plan without mistakes and without errors. Let us also remember that little earth in relation to our own galaxy is so very small in size that it is not one part in ten thousand quintillion quintillion. Our little galaxy is so tiny in relation to the entirety of the manifest universe that we are unable to imagine its relative smallness. Everything—the galaxies, our little earth, the vastness of the universe—is a part of the One Plan of the One Eternal God.

We must also realize that at any given time we are able to understand and enter into our Cosmic Work. True enough, our infant minds cannot comprehend the plan in its entirety. Nor can we realize its scope in terms of physical dimension. However, the Infinite Intelligence has endowed us with the ways and means of determining what to do and how to do it, in order to cooperate in the fulfillment of the Divine Plan as intelligent workers. We have also inherited the free-will choice of determining whether or not we are going to perceive and follow our destined course with a minimum of pain or with a maximum of unnecessary travail.

We are not given a choice as to what we were created for, any more than the earth is given a choice as to the time when surface changes must take place. The Ordinance of Heaven has a time limit on everything that is, ever was or will be. In the case of individual humans, pressures build up until they are somewhat forced—as a measure of self-protection—to look to the light to learn that the old way was the way of error.

One prejudicial taboo is against becoming too genuinely analytical in regard to the presentation of a particular science in which the inquisitor is supposed to be an authority. The student who disagrees too much with some preconceived concept in class, becomes earmarked as a trouble maker and is likely to find his education terminated in a particular institution. The professor's Drive for Significance must not be offended, or unpleasant consequences might follow! They are somewhat like the hell fire awaiting the analytical thinker who offends some religious leader's Drive for Significance by daring to question his wisdom and accuracy.

Of course, such an attitude is the antithesis of a belief in genuine freedom of worship. It is an effort to suppress and distort the facts of life—therefore, subversive in the truest sense. Obviously, a person who has succumbed to brainwashing can be nothing else than a slave to the ideas and errors of the person or group advocating and conducting the washing.

Such a person can become free in the true sense only when he gains understanding of what has happened to him and determines to be a free soul. To do this he must gain understanding of his true relationship to God, to his fellow man, to other life forms, and determine to do his own thinking—no longer allowing a prejudiced mind who knows nothing of astrology or the soul to do his thinking for him. In any case, the controls must be thrown off; the mind and emotions must be cleared for a new source of thought, feeling and action insuring Captaincy of the Soul and Mastership of the Fate.

It is only the individual who has himself attained to true freedom that can contribute to free governments and to the freedom of individual souls.

The perverted Drive for Significance with the attendant desire to dictate is so very common that the person who believes in complete freedom of worship and complete freedom of expression is rather rare, percentagewise. All people believe (so they say) in such freedoms, but observation indicates such belief is limited to self or the group with which self is associated. Too many believe in suppression of view points opposed to their own.

If we are intellectually honest with ourselves, we must accept the following beliefs:

—believe in freedom for all.

—believe in the right of all people in any country to have access to as much accurate information on life—both here and hereafter—as they desire to get at any time.

—believe that all people have the God-given right to expand their consciousness as fast and as far as they desire.

—believe that no person, organization or group has the right to brainwash anyone or to determine for anyone what the relationship is or should be of the individual to all other life forms and to God.

—believe in the right of any person or group to be as intellectually blind and as spiritually stupid as they wish.

But we cannot believe that such persons or groups have the right to force their errors upon anyone else through dictative methods and brainwashing tactics. As free souls we have a right to demand that all people likewise have the right to be free souls if they so desire; that all people have the right to be slaves until such time as they awaken to the glorious realities of life as it is—its multitude of privileges and blessings and the incomparably beautiful vista of Eternal Progression.

Mountains rise and erode away. Continents appear and sink. Civilizations are established and perish. Even planets die and return to disorganized dust. The human soul as part and parcel of Eternal Life, however, goes on through Progressive Evolution to higher and ever higher states of being, the enlightened souls working in self-conscious oneness with Eternal God. Let There Be Light!

USE YOUR MIND

HUMANKIND, being the highest form of physical life, possesses potentials vastly greater than those enjoyed by any other life form upon earth. For a human being to realize and use these limitless potentials, some method must be used to gain knowledge of what they are.

It is just here that astrology comes in, for it is the only tool under the Sun which provides a map of these basic potentials. Basic potentials exist within the soul or subconscious mental organism in the form of basic urges and conditioning energy received up to birth in human form as a result of the evolution of the individual soul or consciousness.

Consequently, in the teachings of our religion, we lay great stress upon this Golden Key (as it was anciently called), for it alone provides the means of unlocking the secrets of the soul and enabling the turner of the key to begin to understand self, the relation of the soul to the universe, to its Creator and to Creation.

To understand astrology and its potential usages requires a study of "Esoteric Psychology"[1] and "Mental Alchemy"[1] as well as the other Alchemies. I have, in the course of the many years since I first contacted the Brotherhood of Light Lessons on the physical plane, known many people who have gained a smattering of astrology and who have made a perfunctory study of the teachings of our religion, but who have never realized that for any information to do any good, it must be put to use in the individual life.

I have also known many who started out on the pathway with an earnest desire to learn all they could about life so that they might gain an understanding of self, the proper relationship of self to other humans and other life forms and the proper relationship of the Whole of the One Life to the Creator we call God. These have made much progress toward self mastery and have been able to understand that each one has an individual purpose in life and an individual responsibility to God and Creation.

[1] By C. C. Zain

PHILOSOPHY

That each life form manifests a soul is ably set forth in "Organic Alchemy."[1] The difference in the life manifested by any creature lesser than the human species is one of degree, not of kind. In each case, it is the manifestation of feeling and intelligence through form.

There are many forces that affect human life during its brief physical tenure. In addition to astrological energies are the thoughts and opinions of others and the efforts by others to control or influence the individual through propaganda. These forces and techniques are set forth in considerable detail in "Imponderable Forces."[1] Unless one understands the methods used to get one to accept false doctrines and statements, it is not possible to analyze the propaganda and arrive at correct conclusions relative to its purpose.

I would suggest that those who have an earnest desire to know more of life, its sources, the energies that affect each individual part of it, and the sources of the energies as well as the methods of operation and laws governing the entire process of the Progressive Evolution of the individual and the Whole, study the entire 21 Courses of Brotherhood of Light Lessons,[1] embracing the Religion of The Stars.

This is because the most intelligent course of action can be selected by the individual soul (you), only when the most comprehensive knowledge is at hand relative to life and its multiplicity of relationships and energies. The earnest seeker needs to know which types of thought, feeling and action are beneficial and which types are destructive.

Such study leads to many realizations including the purpose of being, the origin and destiny of the human soul, of how to learn to love God through learning to understand and love creation. The practice of the principles involved lead to a continually higher level of consciousness until one reaches the divine consciousness and then truly becomes One with God.

All of the foregoing represents effort and demands that one learn to view each successive step as a problem which has one best solution. Then one needs to learn that by associating pleasure with the solution of the problem that life becomes an enjoyable game.

One also needs to learn that the experiences of life can be transmuted into spiritual values by adopting the correct mental attitudes toward them as pointed out in "Spiritual Alchemy."[1]

Above all, one needs to learn that knowledge to be of value must be put into practice in this business of living. Otherwise, it is inactive information creating nothing in the way of a better life because it is inert.

So I would suggest that with all of your getting that you get sufficient understanding to realize that it is what YOU DO that determines whether you function on the brute level or gradually transmute the energies of your soul into the Divine thus realizing your Divine potentials of usefulness,

[1] By C. C. Zain

happiness and spirituality by learning to know yourself, be yourself and give yourself.

In addition to making individual progress, each soul is a member of humanity as a whole. As such, each soul needs to learn how the energies of society might best be channeled toward a realization of God's Great Plan for that society. This entails the study of "Cosmic Alchemy."[1]

Bertrand Russell has been quoted as saying, "Only a few people think, and only a few of those who think they think, actually think." Unfortunate (for the progress of the human race) as such a situation is, it is very nearly the truth of the matter.

The materialist is sure that the five physical senses and reason are adequate, and he denies that there are other senses and other means of information. He also denies that there are degrees of matter and energies that are beyond his present ken. The materialist may be recognized by the world as a scientist. But the fact is that in his self-induced blindness, he is unscientific.

The religious leader who is determined to keep minds enslaved is sure that any information of a life hereafter can only come through his particular church. Such a leader does not advocate individual freedom of the soul and individual determination of the truth of the matter.

Each soul is an independent entity, working out its own salvation. There can only be one primary source of energy, one Creative Power that acts to produce eternal change in existing form in the continuing business of Creation. And since this Power (Energy) we call God has set up laws governing every process—physical, chemical, mental and emotional—there can be only One order of Truth in the universe.

Whatever exists must exist as something and in something. This applies to all things and energies—physical, astral and spiritual. Something may be defined as some sort of energy, matter and motion in some time-space relationship.

The one active principle is energy. Energy must always have some source. Neither energy nor matter can exist in or be taken from nothing. The existence of anything demands a medium in which to manifest. The medium itself demands something else in which to exist. Whenever we admit the existence of anything in which anything takes place, we admit the existence of something serving as matter, and matter is a substance of some degree of fineness made of some sort of particles.

Whether we call the medium for the transmission of radio signals, light, and other radiations "ether" or "field" makes not the slightest difference. The fact remains that it must be something and made of something. The human soul, and for that matter the ego, to be anything must be something. Consequently, they are made of something and affected by some sort of energies, these elements that constitute both the Life and Divine in man,

[1] By C. C. Zain

PHILOSOPHY

come under laws governing substance and energy. "The Laws Of Occultism"[1] goes into the basis of this subject in some detail.

In the last analysis, it is literally impossible for anyone to think and feel for anyone else. Each person is thus an individual soul. Precisely because of this God-given individuality, each soul becomes responsible for its own intellectual and spiritual progression, or stagnation, as the case may be.

The chief energies affecting any human soul are the thoughts and feelings of the individual. It is these individual thoughts and feelings that when properly understood and brought under control enable each soul to direct and channel other energies reaching the soul into constructive channels of expression. This includes all energies from astrological and other sources. It is thus that one learns to rule the stars.

Since this thought and feeling must take place within the individual mental and emotional organism (or soul), a person can only be free of control by others when he accepts individual responsibility. If he prefers to let others determine what he shall think and feel, then he prefers to be a slave rather than a free soul.

In both science and religion, one can find many persons and many groups who are anxious and ready to do one's thinking and make one's decisions, thus limiting the intellectual and spiritual horizon. In neither case is there a genuine concern for either the intellectual or spiritual welfare of the individual. On the contrary, such actions indicate a desire to serve as dictatorial slave masters. In all of cosmos only God is Absolute. All else is relative.

Commonly, egotism is mistaken for dignity; emotional reaction is mistaken for an intellectual process; and feeling is mistaken for thinking. To believe that what one knows is the limit of all knowledge is to forget that honesty requires a recognition of an individual's current limitations.

No living person knows all about matter and energy. No living person knows all about God and Creation. Each individual consciousness, no matter in whose physical body it manifests, is an expanding potential. Even as more and more knowledge is gained, and more and more love and wisdom is manifested, each individual consciousness is still a soul on the pathway that extends through an eternity of time-space relationships, manifesting life in almost numberless degrees of substance and a multitude of degrees of energy in the limitless here and hereafter.

In the life processes of our little planet Earth, mountain chains have been thrust up and eroded away; continents have risen and sunk beneath the seas; and civilizations have arisen and vanished. The Laws of God governing the evolutionary processes of all life and of human souls and human egos were brought into being an eternity ago. They will continue to govern the evolutionary processes in the same eternity that lays ahead of each human soul.

[1] By C. C. Zain

Each soul possesses all of the potentials necessary to understand and find its individual place in this vast Divine Plan. You, as an individual, can choose for yourself whether or not you will recognize that to gain knowledge demands study and analysis, so that the knowledge gained may be applied to developing and using your latent abilities.

Belief is not knowledge. Knowledge is gained by proving and disproving information. The laboratory of life is open to all, and the pages of the infallable Book of Nature are ever open to those who can recognize that God works in, through, and as, Nature.

The limitless Creative Power (Energy) that we call God, and the limitless forms of substance in which this energy manifests that we call Creation, are occult (mysterious) only to those souls who have not perceived as yet their true relationships, or who are unwilling to become free souls and thus captains of their own fate.

The pathway is always open; the doorway is always before each soul; and freedom always awaits the claiming. So it is and ever has been and will ever be.

MAN VERSUS GOD

IN THE January 16, 1962 issue of Look magazine appears an article by J. Robert Moskin, Look's senior editor, headed: "In the next twenty-five years, man will master the secret of creation." The heading over the second page reads: "Will man discover the molecular structure of God?" The article states that man is on the verge of creating life in a test tube since he has discovered DNA and other nucleic acids. Accompanying the article is a picture of a laboratory model of a molecule.[1]

Let us look at the molecule. As do all molecules, it consists of atoms rather widely separated from each other and held in place by an undefined something called adhesion. All adhesion means is that they stick together. In liquid acids, this undefined something behaves in one way. In a piece of wood or other solid, it behaves in another way. In a piece of rubber or other stretchable material, it behaves still another way.

Atoms are all similar to miniature solar systems with wide open spaces between the component parts. In the case of magnetic attraction, the "force" called magnetism acts on the atom as an integral unit just as though it were a solid ball, which according to current conceptions, it is not. Man does not yet know what the force is that holds the atoms together in any molecule, or what the force called magnetism is.

These forces, like gravity, have many peculiarities. For instance, the gravity of our galactic center acts on the entire solar system and its gravity just as though the whole thing was a solid ball. It behaves just like the atoms in relation to magnetic forces.

[1] Many similar references are still found in current literature.

Within the atom and within the solar system, there are wide open spaces and energy fields behaving as solids in relation to magnetic and gravitational forces and the force that holds the atoms in place in molecules. We can say that a force holds the atoms together in a molecule. We can say magnetism is a force and that gravity is a force. But when we have said that much, we have said about all that is known.

The Look article contains many quotes from scientists. One by Pauling says: "There is no reason why nucleic acid, proteins, genes should not be synthesized—why genes should not be introduced into living things."

Such a statement requires the presupposition that all life and memory are but chemical processes. That life does not require the pre-existence of an intelligence with knowledge gained from experience in order to direct the building and animation of the organism.

If this supposition is correct, since the DNA is supposed to be the creative element, then it must naturally follow that in addition to controlling hereditary traits and being the God of living cell as well as the devil (see article) that can kill cells, it is possible to make a chemical synthesis of the entirety of higher education and inject it into the living organism of a child. This process would eliminate the necessity of wasting toilsome years of study to become a good scientist or, for that matter, a magazine editor. Taxpayers would be spared tremendous expense if knowledge could be gained by a hypodermic injection. Absurd, you say? Of course it is, but no more so than calling DNA the designer of life or assuming that man is about to create life from dead matter.

Life is a manifestation of feeling and intelligence through form. The difference between a dead cell—which has exactly the same chemical composition—and a living cell is that the building, controlling and directing intelligence has discarded a physical structure. The cell is dead when the intelligence has left it. It is living while the non-physical intelligence (soul) is using it and directing its functions. Obviously, intelligence and feeling are not molecular structures, atomic structures or the unknown forces that cause atoms to exhibit a certain togetherness in various molecular structures.

Man does not know why one arrangement of molecules is solid when another is not, or what it is that stretches in a rubber band, nor why one material is transparent and another similar material is not. As a matter of fact, matter and the unknown forces and energies that make these differences possible are supernatural. What is known is how to use various materials and energies, and it is in this realm of useage that science has made real progress.

Since life is the manifestation of feeling and intelligence through forms, life is feeling and intelligence, not the form through which it manifests. There is only one kind of life, only one kind of intelligence, and to be able to create life in a test tube, man would first have to create the animating intelligence. This requires the primary false assumption that intelligence is chemical reaction, and the common materialistic assumption that everything arises from gross matter.

The article question "Will man discover the molecular structure of God" implies that God evolved on earth strictly by chance. It also implies that man is capable of analyzing the Supreme Intelligence and reducing Him to a chemical formula. The editor quotes many scientists who make various unwarranted assumptions as the result of some advances in information.

Neither the editor nor the scientists get around to analyzing life or realizing that the pre-requisite to any living thing (physical) is an intelligence ready to take over and animate the particular form when the right physical conditions have been provided. Only after the non-physical intelligence or soul has taken over can anything be called alive. The Super Intelligence we call God, who manifests as Life, Light and Love, who interpenetrates and actively directs all manifestations of energy, matter and motion, and in Whom we Live, Move, Breathe and have our Being, works through a multitude of inner as well as material realms.

So far as science knows anything is solid because God so wills. Atoms are held in place in molecules because God so Wills. The chair you sit on supports you because it is held together by something, and all that the materialists know about it is that it does.

The 1962 Information Please Almanac contains an article by Willie Ley, entitled "What Is Life?" This article does not exhibit the egotism of the Look presentation, but like it, it never gets around to the obvious fact that life is feeling and intelligence manifesting through form. Nor does it recognize the fact that the animation of any physical form requires the pre-existence of the manifesting intelligence.

The Look article reveals how very widespread the false doctrine of materialism has become in our colleges and universities. Since the various mental (psychological) factors necessary to life are completely ignored, it is clearly an attempt, for purposes not stated, to advance materialism, if it is just egotism pretending to knowledge not possessed by the author. In any case, it reveals why those who become the end products of higher education sometimes defect to Communism. They have been conditioned to blindly accept statements on authority, and any latent ability to use the searchlight of critical analysis has been brainwashed out of them.

The Look article also points up the fact that most, if not all, of these scientists and the Editor do not know the difference between egotism and self respect. I submit that it is impossible for a person who has genuine self respect to be egotistical. Such a person recognizes the limitations of his own knowledge and is humble.

It is well to note that the only physical building blocks of matter are the minute particles within the atom, and that the distances between these particles are as great, relatively speaking, as the distances between the planets and sun in our solar system.

Atoms, then, are composed of wide open spaces and minute particles. Yet in a molecule something holds the atoms in place. This something behaves in various ways, but is obviously made of something else. What this adds up to is that matter consists of a few sub-microscopic particles and a vast area of wide open spaces—made of nothing at all according to present physical concepts. Until the theory of a sub-electronic-sub-field (ether) substance and energy is adopted, no reason at all can be advanced for anything about matter and its various behavior patterns.

Because the area of ignorance is so great and the area of knowledge is so small, no living man has cause to think he can do something with matter that will enable him to emulate or supplant God. Jumping to conclusions is not thinking. Indeed, in looking over the Look article to examine in detail the various statements attributed to the various scientists, I wonder if their concept of DNA isn't just a bit addled in some of their thought-cells.

If we consider the article as an essay on life, it adds up to drivel. It is not particularly scientific or intelligent to try to reduce God to the status of a bunch of Amino Acids and down to the size of a single-celled creature. It is not scientific or intelligent to consider a molecule with the wide open spaces between the component atoms and completely disregard the force that holds the atoms in place. It is not intelligent or scientific to imagine (albeit vainly) that because man has made a little minor headway, relatively speaking, that he is on the verge of playing God.

I repeat that in a cell that has just died because the animating intelligence (soul) has finished using it as a means of gaining experience with relative conditions, the chemical compounds—including DNA—are identical with the components of the same cell when alive. The DNA does not create life but is subject to the forces of decay and dissolution. Consequently, the life is in the animating intelligence and not in the physical structure of the cell.

Because it is just this same type of thinking used by the Soviet in attempting to expound atheism and brainwash its peoples into blind acceptance, I find it necessary to take the time, energy and space to point out a few of the facts.

Hitler gave the world an example of unbridled egotism and its accompanying insanity.

A newspaper editor wrote me some years ago, "Man starts out with the primary false assumption that something is known. The truth is that nothing is known."

Perhaps it would do these microscopic scientists some good to take a few telescopic looks at the universe and contemplate the power and the glory of the God that created it and all of its multitude of suns and other bodies and the forces keeping law and order on such a grand scale. I doubt that any one of them, including Look's editor, would ask, "Will man discover the molecular structure of gravity?"

What, then is one to think of the question: Will man discover the molecular structure of God? Genes and chromosomes notwithstanding, the soul of man is not a physical structure of chemical composition. Like the intelligence that animates a single cell, it must preexist in order to animate the human form. It is non-physical and survives physical death.

When little man is still so ignorant of matter and its formation and does not know how or why a chair supports his weight, he is indeed suffering from egomania to the point of dementia when he presumes he is about to create life, or assumes that he is going to reduce the God of all the galaxies comprising the Cosmos to the status of a virus and put Him in a tube.

The much higher frequency (and smaller-particled) worlds of the Inner Planes offer unlimited opportunities for research and exploration. This is the realm of the subconscious mental organism or soul. It is the reservoir of memory and the realm of intuition and, on the higher levels, of inspiration. It is in this inner realm that man can and often does contact God directly, through prayer.

Even if some chemist succeeded in providing just the right conditions for life to manifest, he still would not create life, for the animating intelligence would have to come from somewhere outside of the nucleic acids.

The ability to organize and direct the functions within any organism, from the single cell to the human form, must of necessity be the result of experience gained in building and directing still other less complex forms. Intelligence does not spring automatically into being in this respect, any more than it springs automatically into being in the outside world in which physical forms function.

Experience is necessary to learn to do anything. In study we review the experiences of others even as we gain experience of our own, adding the total to our memory. We act upon and react to the information gained in both ways in the business of living. Our intelligence is measured by the ability we gain to form new, independent and correct conclusions from the data at hand.

If we jump to unwarranted conclusions, or try to present what we think we know in a false light, in order to satisfy our Drive for Significance, we are not being intelligent or doing real thinking. On the contrary we are behaving as the small boy trying to attract attention to himself, running around and yelling, "Look at me!"

Within God's gradually unfolding plan of progressive evolution of consciousness, man will progress to a continually greater understanding of life and its functions, including the relationship of the individual soul to the Creator. Eternal progress is the Anthem of Creation, and unless in the insanity of his egotism, man eliminates himself and leaves the earth to the microbes, the vistas of the future hold many undreamed of (at present) discoveries.

Man will never create life. He will ultimately come to the understanding that all life is One, providing he divests himself of his egotism and begins to lift himself above the brute level of intelligence. He will in time make sufficient spiritual progress to realize that there is only One primary source of all Energy, Matter and Motion and all Life, Light and Love.

EXPERIENCE: THE TEACHER

WE MOVE about in these bodies of ours without much thought as to how we came to possess them, or as to how our souls gained the ability to construct so complex an organism as the human form.

Yet there is no mystery connected with the process if we but look about us and perceive nature in operation, the means by which it is possible. Perhaps the reader has perceived that all of us are children going to school for the purpose of learning such lessons as will enable us to advance to higher Astral and Spiritual Realms upon the completion of this little grade and to become useful citizens of Cosmos. At least it is the hope of this writer that all of them have made that much progression.

Have you ever pondered upon the problem connected with the caterpillar and the butterfly? The intelligence or soul that directs the building of the body of the caterpillar gains sufficient experience in the process that it is enabled through this knowledge plus what it gains in contact with environment through this form to build the vastly more complex body of the butterfly from the same substance which comprised the body of the caterpillar, which to all intents and purposes suffered physical death and disintegration.

This new structure enables the soul to gain a much wider range of experience than was possible while functioning through the body of the caterpillar, and to cover more territory in a single day than could the slow moving caterpillar during its entire lifetime. This observation of nature at work through natural law is an experience of immense value to the sincere seeker for Truth, for but little thought will convince him that the same law applies to the human soul as applies to that of the caterpillar.

The soul of man does not spontaneously learn how to construct the human body any more than the soul of the caterpillar knew without experience in building a lesser form, how to construct the more complex organism of the butterfly. The human form is constructed by its directing intelligence or soul—solely because of experience gained in constructing lesser life forms, retaining from each as memory, the knowledge so gained and the ability to carry through the life processes such as assimilation, secretion, etc., without conscious direction.

Through such observations we are able to perceive that experience is the teacher which enables souls to make progression and that without such experience there would be no consciousness and no progression of souls.

A study of the history of life and its evolutionary phases in some of our large natural history museums will show the student that there were once many varieties of life upon earth that are now extinct, because they were unable to adapt themselves to the ever-changing environmental conditions brought about by the life processes of the physical earth.

This, too, teaches us the lesson that the soul to continue to express life in any phase of existence must adapt itself to the exigencies of the environment in which it functions. The penalty for failure exacted by the laws of nature, which are God's laws, is physical extinction. And to the inhabitants of any plane of expression, the substance of that plane is physical and that of which the bodies are constructed.

Observing nature in manifestation, we are also forced to the conclusion that in time the earth, too, will finish its life processes and pass away, the substance undergoing disintegration and passing back into the energy fields of space. When this takes place, electromagnetic and astral planes will in time follow this process, leaving only the eternal spiritual substance, and unless there is a recognition of adaption to higher conditions than physical and astral planes, the remaining souls will disintegrate and pass along with the other substance back into the energy fields—the only way a soul could possibly be lost.

Science has a rather clear-cut exposition of the progress of physical life on earth up to and including the manlike ape, or apelike man as you prefer. It fails, however, to find the missing link, and this is also because it fails to apply the basic law of physics to the problem of evolution and recognize that for every such period there must of necessity also be a period of involution.

The key to the point of meeting of these periods can be found in the story in the Sixth Chapter of Genesis. In universal symbolism, the same story is expressed by the two trines meeting on a plane surface, as seen in The Church of Light Emblem.

In order to express higher states of consciousness the soul must of necessity have experiences in expressing lower states of consciousness, just as to build a higher life form it must have experience in building lower life.

God, through nature, has provided the means by which the soul can gain experience and knowledge sufficient to construct these higher forms and thus make progress through gaining increased perceptions, and after this phase to start the journey back to Celestial Realms and the Angelic Form.

In each higher phase, the soul expresses life more vividly, gaining knowledge, experiencing pleasure and pain as it adapts to or fails to meet the conditions of the environment in which it functions.

The motivating force behind each life form is its Divine Ego, which is a pure scintillating spark of Deity that has been impressed by its Angelic Parents with the function to be performed in the Divine Plan of Cosmic Construction. The ego, in turn, evolves the twin souls that are represented in the Angelic State by the double-headed golden eagle of Masonry and starts the souls out on the involutionary and evolutionary journeys through the Cycle of Necessity to gain such experience and knowledge as will enable them to enter into their ultimate function as intelligent workers in the cosmic structure.

One cannot be self-centered and progress to Spiritual Realms. Selfishness must be left behind and wholehearted sincere work done in behalf of the cosmic whole must be undertaken and done if such heights are to be reached. Knowledge must be gained of the relationship of the soul to Deity and to all other life forms, if mortality is to be attained.

By your experiences you can gain the knowledge which applied with wisdom will enable your soul to make progress up the spiral of life to Angelic Realms. Experience is the teacher which you must heed in order to gain these exalted heights.

THE DIVINE IMAGE

THE ALL inclusive, intelligent, all loving, all living Creative Being we call God is the builder, energizer and active director of His Kingdom. This Kingdom includes the physical solar systems and countless billions of galaxies that make up the Universal Whole of physical matter and energy. It also includes the entirety of astral, spiritual and celestial energy and matter.

The sub-rulers of this kingdom we call angels and arch angels, spiritual beings of the life beyond the grave and others who have perceived their relationship to and function in this vast Divine Plan. The continually moving and changing form of mind and matter proclaims a progressive evolution taking place within the Eternal Whole of The Kingdom of God.

Man has a spiritual ego or god within, the energizing force driving his soul to gain experience within the ever changing environmental conditions brought about by the progressive evolution of the Whole.

Man also has a soul (his mental organism, subconscious and conscious) and a body. His attitudes shown by his habit systems of thought, feeling and action constantly create the circumstances and conditions of his individual life here and hereafter.

Atoms and cells in the organic structures of his body have independent intelligences working away as sub-rulers in his Microcosmic Kingdom, precisely as the Macrocosmic God has sub-rulers working away in Creation as a Whole. The difference in function between Microcosmic and Macrocosmic God is one of degree rather than kind.

Few of mankind have as yet realized that they are a god in the sense that they are creating happiness or misery for themselves, using the powers they have been given by a beneficent God. Whether the soul is drifting aimlessly upon the sea of life, striking a rock here or a reef there, and occasionally running into emotional storms; or whether the individual soul has recognized its true nature and realized that man is, in truth, made in the image and likeness of God, depends upon the amount of accurate information gained and upon the intelligence with which the individual has attempted to become "Captain of his soul and Master of his fate."

Like God, man lives in Eternity. And like God, man is eternally creating through utilizing his creative powers of thought, feeling and action. The entire future of the Whole is contained as a potential within the Whole and will be brought into being by the ceaseless creative thinking, feeling and acting of God. Likewise, the entire future of Microcosmic man is contained, as a potential, in the sphere of man consisting of Ego, Soul and Body functioning and evolving with the aid of his creative powers of thinking, feeling and acting.

In truth, man was created in the image and likeness of God, and in his infinite love and wisdom, the one and only God gave to man the power to create his own destiny as a Microcosm functioning within the Macrocosm we call God.

In this plan of creation God also insured the eventual evolution of the consciousness of man to the point that each would perceive and take up his task as a cooperative part of the Divine Plan, either here or hereafter—depending upon the individual. God also insured that all attempts of the individual to escape the responsibility for his own creations of happiness or misery would end in failure. For God did not give to man the ability to interfere with His Plan of Eternally Progressive Evolution, of which the individual is a very small but necessary part.

It is impossible for anyone to run away from one's own thoughts and feelings, and thus impossible to abdicate the throne of his own kingdom. Each must learn to accept the inescapable fact that he is truly made in the image and likeness of God. Like God, he is a ruler and creator within his own lesser sphere, making his life a heaven or hell by the activities of his own creative powers of thought, feeling and action.

Realizing this, one can understand the tremendous power of each soul to direct its own destiny and the limitless potential that each possesses through using directed thinking and induced emotion.

To know yourself, to be yourself as a constantly evolving better self, and to give yourself in unselfish service to other life forms, thus assisting the progressive evolution of the Divine Whole, is to practice The Religion of The Stars.

When one becomes impatient, it is time to recall that the God who created man in His own image lives and works in Eternity, that working in Eternity the task is never finished, and that this God is not in a hurry. Since God is not in a hurry, it behooves little man—because he is made in the image of God—to also cultivate patience, and realize that his job of creating a better and more Divine Selfhood will also never be finished, for man also lives in Eternity.

To study The B. of L. and apply the teachings to the task of gaining knowledge of self and learning the techniques and applying the principles of directed thinking and induced emotion in order to enfranchise the soul from its bonds of error and emotional disorder is to begin the task of freeing the soul. To become a good Captain one must learn something of Navigation. Our task is to provide the raw material for this education.

GOD AND YOU

GIVE ME Thy hands, holding Thy Spirit, that I may receive It and live by It. It is my desire that I may hear Thy voice, that my body may be rejuvenated with life through love of Thee. Give my Thy hands, holding Thy Spirit, that I may receive It and live by It and give life unto others.

Containing the whole secret of self help through prayer, the above is attributed to Akhenaten, the King of Egypt who ascended to the throne in 1375 B. C., and who at nineteen years of age contacted the same spiritual sources from which the current presentation of the Religion of The Stars emanages. The secret is contained in the phrase "and give life unto others."

If a prayer is wholly selfish and based upon a desire to get without giving, it cannot reach higher than those astral realms inhabited by selfish souls. On the contrary, when the idea of prayer is to gain help in order to assist others, then it is wholly unselfish and can, with sufficiently intense desires to work with God in the fulfillment of the Divine Plan, reach God directly and bring one for a time in contact with the highest of all.

When one has labored with unselfish intelligence and is sufficiently grateful to God for the opportunity to work in collaboration with Him in the fulfillment of His Plan, then true Illumination becomes possible. It is through this Illumination that one realizes that while the operation of the Laws of God are impartial and impersonal, God is at one and the same time a very Personal God. A God capable of being contacted directly by each Human Soul who fulfills the Law.

The individual who has contacted God directly and experienced the indescribable ecstacy that floods the entire being has obtained first hand knowledge of the Divine Origin and Destiny of the Soul of Man. Such an individual does not need any convincing as to the immortality of life, for he has gained Self Conscious Immortality and the positive knowledge that his Spiritual Ego and the Spiritual God are indeed ONE.

A candidate for this type of initiation in the Grand Lodge of the Universe must strip himself of all illusion and self importance as a physical being. He must take off the garb of false values induced by a materialistic conception of life. He must stand naked before the Treasurer (his divine soul) of the Lodge and know that in order to make a deposit he must understand and use Spiritual Values.

A neophyte who has selected the Spiritual Pathway will not find it without obstacle, for the means of testing the sincerity and strength of the resolution is at hand in the form of the untransmuted desires of his own animal soul. When the desires are transmuted and he no longer mistakes the dross of appearances for Spiritual Gold, then his desires are truly Divine and form part of the Divine Soul. It is the usage of the energies in a wholly unselfish manner that raises the frequency level from the lower astral to the realms of Spiritual Light.

The untransmuted desires of the animal soul are the rough ashlar, or unpolished diamond, of Ancient Masonic lore. The ultimate goal of the Divine Soul (in this Cycle of Necessity) is to unite with its mate in the angelic form, so well symbolized by the double-headed Golden Eagle of Masonic lore.

The attainment of Angelhood is referred to in Revelations as "the marriage of the lamb," and it is referred to as the accomplishment of the Great Work in Ancient Masonry, by C. C. Zain. This state of Angelhood marks the end of one great cycle and the beginning of a new one. Throughout the journey, the direction of travel is always toward the Light.

That light is symbolized by the East in Ancient Masonry, the direction of the rising of the physical sun. The Spiritual Sun is God; the source of all Spiritual Light (understanding), the source of Spiritual Love, and the source of all Life.

During the course of his spiritual education, the neophyte is called upon to continually expand his intellectual horizon, to continually refine his emotions, and to make unceasing progress toward self mastery. He has to learn how to use directed thinking and induced emotion in order to function more and more efficiently in his self selected task of working with God in the fulfillment of the Divine Plan.

To be one of the called and chosen is a privilege granted by the Creator to each human soul. No one is left out in the call. The choosing is, however, left up to each individual soul. Whether one strays by the wayside or con-

continues in the straight and narrow pathway towards the Spiritual Light is dependent upon the individual. One must learn to deposit the refined gold of the Spirit with the treasurer of the lodge in order to experience the measureless blessings of true Divine Consciousness and the exstacies of true illumination, wherein the individual and his God are ONE in the highest sense of the word.

"Many are called but few are chosen" is entirely true of the humans inhabiting little earth. Most people must await a considerable amount of experience in the next life in astral realms before they realize there is no vicarious atonement or attainment. It is because a great majority of all peoples of the earth embrace, quite blindly, a philosophy which advocates some escapist method of using a scapegoat, that most peoples are not chosen.

God has provided a door that can be opened whenever one knocks in the right manner and uses the correct password. The door opens upon comprehensive information as to the real nature of the human soul and its true relationship to God and the Creation that is the manifestation of God.

The correct password is the realization that Goodness alone is Power, and that to be truly Good one must become spiritually wise. With this equipment, one is prepared to start upon the spiral pathway that leads to the crowning glory of human potential—Angelhood while yet in the flesh, full and conscious angelic union with the soul mate.

Healing Prayer

O Thou Eternal Spirit, in Whom we Live, Move, Breathe and have our Being! As Brethren of the Light we seek health at the fountain of Thy abundance. We ask that out of Thy goodness and power, health may come to each individual here listed and here gathered. We ask this that we may better assist as constructive workmen in realizing Thy Great Evolutionary Plan.

By virtue of our unselfishness and sincerity in desiring to assist in Thy works, we ask, while we remain a few minutes in silence, that Ministers of Thine direct the healing energies so that all those listed and all those gathered here, may have and live in perfect health.

(A few minutes of silence)

Closing Prayer:

O Thou Eternal One! From our hearts we thank Thee for thus bestowing Thy blessing of health upon us.

So Shall It Be!

Psychology and Alchemy

II.

PROPER PERSPECTIVE

SETTING side by side are three houses. One is built of granite, one of wood and one is a thatch house of straw. These houses represent spiritual values, intellectual values and material values in the order given. Almost anyone, if asked to make a choice as to which he would select if he could, would take the house built of enduring stone, because it is the strongest and lasts so much longer. Yet in actual experience, most people choose the straw house of material values as the most important—forgetting completely that only spiritual possessions are eternal.

So, most people impress their subconscious minds with the fact that they do not desire to build a spiritual establishment for the soul and thus attain self-conscious immortality. So the destructive habit of rationalizing is formed, and anything that promises to interfere with the desire to gain material advantage is automatically rejected by the subconscious mind.

As is evidenced by the three houses we use to illustrate the point, the sense of values is misplaced because the progress of the soul is inhibited. Nothing of spiritual value is being deposited in the cosmic bank from which to draw when this transitory physical existence is finished. The real truths of life can only be determined when the neophyte digs deep beneath the rubbish of appearance. It is upon the basis of real truth that true values can be determined.

Whether the problem is a matter of determining the relative importance of spiritual intellectual or material values; a matter of determining the correct relationship to other individuals or events; or a matter of determining just what one should do under a given set of conditions, the dominant desire must be to see the facts as they are, because the progress of the soul is of paramount value.

Whether the sense of values is based upon full consideration of the spiritual, astral and physical nature of the individual, or whether it is based only on the physical is determined by each soul for the individual possessing it. The sense of values is always a matter of self determination.

A person who is always trying to be clever and outsmart his fellow humans seldom has either the time or desire to be intelligent. True intelligence demands a full consideration of all of the factors entering into any problem, and particularly the problem of determining correct relationships and correct values.

The human soul and its divine ego has potentials far beyond the ability of most to even imagine. It is part of the tradition of our teachings that each immortal pair of souls (Male and Female) united in the angelic form constitutes the seed of a future universe. Even so, there are, and always will be, a multitude of other universes, actively presided over and energized and directed by the Supreme Intelligence we call God.

Being finite, the human soul cannot become infinite. Thus the soul with its Ego and form may (and does) partake of all of the attributes of God. However, it is not and can never become God.

The real truths of spiritual, astral and physical life are quite sufficient when understood in the potential for unlimited progress to satisfy the most ambitious seeker after station and honor. Those who spend their time and effort trying to obtain what they imagine is significance through purely physical means—such as amassing much of the world's goods at the expense of others, or attempting to rise to physical station and honor through tearing down others—completely miss the spiritual boat.

Many years ago, a friend of ours who was halfway between the straw and wood houses in choice came to see us. He was the manager of a paper company. That day one of his trucks carrying a load of paper had been ditched. He was much perturbed about the incident.

"It is foolish to worry about business," we told him.

"But," he replied, "I have to worry about my business."

"Just what would happen," we asked, "if you lost that job and didn't get another?"

"I don't know."

"You might have to sell your automobile and furniture in order to eat."

"Yes," he answered, "I guess I would."

"Then, if you did not get a job, you might have to move out on the beach and build a shack," we told him. "And live off of fish and swamp cabbage (the bud of the cabbage palmetto)."

"Yes, I guess I might."

"It would be the best thing that ever happened to you, for then you would have to think."

We went on to explain why. He never forgot the conversation. The chief energies and time were devoted to building a house of straw and almost none to building the house of enduring stone.

We have met others who go to the extreme of building a beautiful rose-tinted cloud in which they imagine they are being spiritual. All of their attention and energy is centered on the beautiful illusory image they hold. Many of these make such statements as "I don't read the newspapers or listen to the news on the radio because there is so much discord." The whole of the physical is regarded as of no value, and as a consequence a completely worthless life is led.

Several years ago, a lady attended a lecture by a noted swami. After the lecture, she cornered the swami and recited a long list of the things she had never done, evidently thinking she had been spiritual. Finally, she paused and asked, "Swami, what should I do?"

"Madame, for God's sake, do something."

All planes of life have a value. One cannot live a physical existence without physical sustenance. There is nothing basically spiritual in either riches or poverty. These, in themselves, are states of physical being which provide experiences, from which the soul—by taking the correct attitudes—can gain spiritual values, or by incorrect attitudes mistake the rubbish of materialism for the priceless gold of spiritual values.

One day we visited a friend who owns a large stationary store. "You know," he said, "when I get time, I'm going to study the Brotherhood of Light lessons."

"You have twenty-four hours in your day," we replied. "No living person has any more or any less. It isn't the time you have, but what you do with it that counts."

Apparently this trend holds for many who have adopted the habit system of procrastination in order to escape facing the realities of individual responsibility.

Another lady related a long story to us of things she had done for God. Then she told of what she expected God to do for her in return. She had not made any effort to ascertain what God wanted her to do or to be. Consequently, she was laboring under the illusion (a rather common one) that she could dictate terms to God. She had not faced the facts of life and all of her demands on God had to do with building straw houses.

No matter how much one tries to deceive self or others, the only pathway up the spiritual heights is the pathway with the realities of the Eternal Truths of God's Law. Every soul that attains the heights must learn, above all else, to seek the unvarnished truth relative to self in relation of physical, astral and spiritual life. Then one should determine, upon the basis of truth, to learn to work consciously with God in the fulfillment of the Divine Plan.

This approach entails learning to love all of creation, to think kindly of all people, to completely lay aside personal ambitions in order to attain spiritual ends. Learning to live a life surrendered to the Divine Will.

In the course of becoming an adept, one will encounter many people connected with many groups who are willing to discourse upon just how the affairs of the world and the universe should be run. These collossal egotists apparently imagine they know better than the Creator what should be done. Be that as it may, God is infinitely more qualified than any finite being to determine what he wants. It is, therefore, a very good plan to study what God does in his progressively evolving plan, in order to determine what is wanted.

The one and only valid reason for feeling proud is when some job is well done. In particular, proud of doing a good task which in some manner assists in making life a little richer or a little finer for some fellow being or beings. The attainment of spiritual station and honor is dependent upon developing the ability to contribute something of value to Universal Welfare, and then doing it.

We know several who have studied the entire Twenty-one Brotherhood of Light Courses (and on occasion received a letter asking, "What should I study now?"), who have never realized that the material contained therein—in order to be of value to the individual—must be put into practice.

When principles are realized and techniques grasped, if the only result is inaction and no effort is made to practice The Religion of The Stars, nothing of value is gained. The house may be of wood, but the stone mansion is not yet possible.

The various teachings presented by The Church of Light, or by any other organization, are of no value to anyone who does not practice them. In order to practice the Religion of The Stars all destructive habit systems need replacement with constructive habit systems.

Regardless of the amount of study one has undergone and regardless of physical accomplishment in building straw houses, the soul is in deepest spiritual ignorance that does not realize that continual character changes are required to attain spiritual advancement. As new abilities are gained, the responsibilities are added to exercise them in the interest of universal welfare. This exercise of ability is the one method by which the development and refinement of the soul can be insured.

Skill in anything is attained only by practice. One of the best means of determining whether or not progress is being made in overcoming the obstacles to spiritual progress presented by faulty habit systems of reacting discordantly to stimuli is through natal astrology. When one no longer reacts discordantly to squares and oppositions as mapped by major directions and the basic predispositions as indicated by the birth chart, one may be sure that a degree of conversion has been accomplished and the character refined. Natal astrology offers the only means by which stimuli can be predetermined and plans made for correcting the habit systems of reacting before the indicated stimuli is present. Thus, natal astrology is a tool of tremendous value to the earnest neophyte who sincerely desires to climb the ladder of spiritual attainment.

If, as is often the case, astrology is only used as a scapegoat, upon whose horns the individual's failure to recognize and attain spiritual treasures is hung, then the misusage of astrology is a detriment to progress.

If a person using astrology is so lacking in spiritual perception that only bad can be seen in the chart, if information gleaned from a chart is put to some destructive use, then the old saying "the undevout occultist is mad" is worthy of attention. What should be looked for in a chart of another is the means by which the particular soul in question can be aided to more successfully adapt to the realities of life as it is—physically, astrally and spiritually.

One's personal disappointments in some department of life may develop a phobia if he is not spiritually inclined. Let us say the personal disappointment concerned marriage. Such a person will try to use marriage charts to condemn the institution of marriage as a whole. If no better use can be found for a practice that has so much potential for good than that, the person using the method—for the benefit of his own soul—should abandon the useage of astrology.

When one studies astrology as an aid to learning the facts of life about himself and as an aid in spiritual development, then it may truly be called a Divine Science. Like everything else, astrology has the potential of being used for good or ill. To retard or assist souls, as the case may be. The same may be said for psychology, which when properly considered is best used as a branch of astrology.

It would be impossible for any person who has attained a degree of adeptship to seek to harm another, for he realizes that the type of thought and feeling associated with the desire to harm retards the progress of the soul.

Each candidate for soul initiation will, however, find that it is sometimes necessary to use quite drastic measures to prevent someone from harming another, or doing something that would retard (if the attempt is successful) the progress of the evolution of the human race. On these occasions the individual is tested to the utmost, for the action taken should (if spiritually considered) be completely impersonal—without anger or the desire for revenge. In these cases, the only spiritually legitimate desire is the desire to protect against those who work—consciously or unconsciously—on the side of the forces of darkness and in opposition to The Legions of Light.

Spiritual values (even as stone houses) do not indicate weakness or supine surrender to anything that may come along. On the contrary, when properly considered, they indicate resistance to evil, protection of the weak and a fortress capable of withstanding the rigors of an ever changing combination of forces, to which the earnest neophyte must constantly adapt.

In event one is so spiritually impoverished that the house of straw seems to be the desirable habitation, then many bitter experiences await the soul—here and hereafter—until the desire is born to face up to the facts of life and start to be of some use to God in order to justify living. For such poor souls, little can be done until a real awakening takes place. It is in this category that one finds those deluded creatures who try to run away from themselves through suicide, or other means such as narcotics.

However, in God's Great Plan, there are no errors of Creation. Ultimately, each soul will find and fill its place. The educational system is so designed that experiences of a given type are repeated until the obvious lesson is gained. No soul is ever lost.

Then there are those who imagine that cold intellect is the answer to problems, and that the mind of embodied human alone is capable of solving all of the problems of the individual. These concentrate the entire attention on the wood house and fail—quite as completely as the devotees of straw-house tactics—to perceive the facts of eternal life.

Intelligence demands that all of the laws and factors entering into any problem be considered. Cleverness always disregards facts. Intelligence, never. Life is the expression of the Will of God; manifesting as Love and Wisdom through a multitude of forms; as God, Macrocosm, and Man, Microcosm; and manifesting in other varieties of expression in the limitless degrees of space-time and substance of the Absolute. Each segment of physical, astral and spiritual life has a purpose related to each other segment and is inseparable from it. When all factors are considered, a correct viewpoint becomes possible.

To attain a properly balanced sense of values and make possible an optimum of real benefits, the neophyte should ever strive to keep everything in a proper perspective. In order to do this, he will learn in time to try to value everything on all planes of expression by weighing it in the scales balanced by a correct sense of values on one hand and the amount that will be contributed to universal welfare on the other.

Properly considered, the beautiful gems of unvarnished truth far outshine the tawdy jewelry of appearances, for they lead the way to spiritual values and to the union of the individual will to the Will of God.

CHANGE DEMANDS PROGRESS

EACH PERSON has a separate set of values, primarily based upon the hereditary drives for Significance, Race Preservation and Self Preservation. Attachment to or for any person, cause or thing, and, conversely, prejudice against any person, cause or thing, is determined by acquired values.

attachment for the past to such an extent that they worship people (who were called masters) and teachings of the past. Then the past becomes sacred, and the masters are viewed as possessing all knowledge and wisdom. This view is accepted without realizing that the only true value of a past teaching lies in a person's ability to adapt its principles to the solution of many present problems. To evolve to a continually higher level of consciousness, man must adjust in an ever changing environment. And nothing on or off the earth is so sacred or untouchable that it cannot be analyzed and applied to some problem.

Occasionally an orthodox devotee will make a fetish of a sacred (to them) book, never realizing that the book itself is composed of paper and ink, and that its true value can be acquired only by putting its principles and teachings into practice here and now. Such worship stems from the desire to satisfy the Drive for Significance by associating with something deemed great rather than with the common practical aspects of personal attainment. Because these worshipful attitudes do not advance one to any higher intellectual or spiritual level, such attempts at satisfying the Drive for Significance are doomed to failure.

When the worshipper is shown the inevitable results of holding such an attitude, usually his first reaction is anger, unless he desires truth above all else. He sees red because he construes the action as an attack upon his station and honor. Then anger is followed by fear—fear that the expose of a false set of values might lose him station and honor. Fear of making an error is also based upon fear of losing station and honor.

Astrologically, the Drive for Significance is chiefly mapped by the Sun in a birth-chart; the Drive for Race Preservation, by Mars; and the Drive for Self Preservation, by Saturn. The correct action necessary to satisfy these three drives can be determined by a comprehensive study of the birth chart. When the basic compounds of the unconscious mind are determined in this manner, their combinations—harmonious or discordant—can be studied to select a control technique which will help the native to establish a correct set of values for himself.

In the academic world, there was and is, a predisposition to make a fetish of the term "science," just as there was and is a tendency to make a fetish of a particular book in the religious world. When something has been commonly designated as a science, it is often worshiped blindly— accepted with all of its faults, just as any religious tenet or doctrine out of the past may be worshiped. When an outsider dares point to an accepted and worshiped error, reactions of members in the sacred reservation (the few true scientists excepted) are identical with reactions of not-supposedly-so-learned persons making a fetish of something different.

Some years ago desiring to know if we had a chance to become a scientist, we asked the editor of a highly respected scientific magazine to define a scientist. The best definition he could give was, "Anyone who has a degree." Sometime later while visiting a friend—an eminent scientist, educator and astronomer—we discussed the possibility of anyone actually knowing nothing yet getting a degree by using recognized authority as the basis for all necessary papers to be prepared. He stated, "Yes, I know many who got their degrees that way."

We have preserved a letter from a Stellar Astronomy textbook author, who knew of our interest in astrology, and one passage of it states, "The one (astronomy) is not quite so white as it has been painted and the other (astrology) is not so black as it has been painted." This letter came after we had won from another eminent astronomer an agreement with our criticism of the above mentioned textbook.

Through the years we have had much correspondence with scientists—real ones and some who just held degrees. When an error was pointed out to them, the real ones who had inadvertently accepted some degree of prejudice did not hesitate to change an erroneous opinion. Some of them even got curious about astrology and learned to do their own thinking on the subject.

An eminent scientist once wrote, "There should be a sign over the entrance to all physics laboratories stating: Philosophical Minds Keep Out. Structural Changes In Progress." Perhaps that sign should appear in other laboratories as well as in mausoleums where outworn ideas and tenets are kept. It is only through change that progress is made. To discard an idea proven false is just as important to the true occult scientist as to acquire a new idea which might be proven true. Mental baggage having no practical use hinders expansion of consciousness. Holding an idea because someone else did or does, is to surrender to that person the right to dictate what progress one may make.

The attitude of blindly accepting without question is the greatest bar to soul progress. Such an attitude is termed uncritical mysticism. When the same attitude is adopted in academic institutions, it is termed authority worship. We recall a physics professor in a junior college who could accurately quote and follow all the formulae in the textbooks, but who was unable to intelligently discuss fundamental theories—a tragic victim of parrot education. Fortunately for the progress of the world, there are a good many other genuine physicists who do not succumb to false idol worship embraced in all forms of authoritarianism.

The only station and honor of value in the Divine Plan is attained by genuine intellectual and spiritual progress and in doing some good work assisting universal welfare. Each soul's mission is to acquire love and wisdom leading to self conscious immortality and to cooperate with all other enlightened souls in furthering eternal progression.

Anyone, if asked, "Do you want to be happy?" would answer, "I do."

Yet many people are reluctant to make changes within themselves to achieve happiness. The truly happy person is one who has developed a harmonious set of reactions toward other people, events and circumstances in daily living. This implies that to some degree the person has a set of values allowing a considerable satisfaction for the three urgent drives within.

Another method of satisfying the Drive for Significance to attain a fancied station and honor is trying to make something appear small by comparison to that associated with self. This practice leads to prejudice. In human life its most primitive expression can be found in the youth who tells his pal, "My dad can lick your dad!" These prejudices express through anger and fear, the first reactions of an offended Drive for Significance. Such prejudices form the basis for destructive propaganda, often leading to physical violence.

Inevitably, each individual must learn to accept full responsibility for his own thoughts, feelings and actions, because no other person can possibly think, feel and act for him. Prejudice indicates ignorance. Attempting to foist these prejudices upon others, or to in any manner dictate their thoughts, feelings and actions, is to practice subversion by trying to enslave and deny the freedom of self expression, thus freedom of soul progress.

Truth—the reality of one's relation to others and to God—alone can make one free. It does not come through the blind acceptance of authority; such blind acceptance effectively bars progress. The teaching of prejudices as truth (including prejudice against astrology) is a subversive practice, for it is an effort to prevent minds from recognizing the propounder's abysmal ignorance as well as the actual facts that can be found in an impartial investigation of the subject (such as astrology). Because the progress of any nation depends upon its citizens' ability to progress intellectually, such teachings may be as dangerous as the equally false, subversive doctrines and hatreds of Communism and Fascism.

It would be an over-simplification, of course, to assume this article embraces all factors involved in human reactions. A very detailed explanation of the basic urges and inner drives will be found in *Esoteric Psychology,* and *Mental Alchemy,* by C. C. Zain. By assimilating and applying the teachings presented in these two courses, any soul will be enabled to speed his spiritual progress.

If we are to be truly Free Souls (as we will eventually be), we must work out our own destiny in accordance with Divine Law. Becoming consciously useful members of Cosmos, working to build a new and better civilization to walk with God insures true happiness through satisfying constructively the three hereditary drives.

Each can and must gain the heights of spiritual attainment for himself, depending upon himself for his own emancipation or Freedom of Soul. To each his own choice in acquiring a set of values.

EVOLVING CONSCIOUSNESS

DESIRING to know the academic viewpoint on memory, I wrote a series of questions dealing with the energy potentials involved and sent them to a number of our leading universities. All kinds of replies were received, most of them expressing a purely material view and, in my opinion, a not too genuinely scientific view.

One, however, was so outstanding in its honesty that it bears quoting: "The electrical theory of the memory trace is obviously invalid, and the later chemical theory presupposes the electrical. I think, therefore, that the progress of science can best be served at the present time by having the courage to admit that no present physical theory can account for the memory trace." This quote from an eminent psychologist is an indication of progress away from the materialistic viewpoint.

When one considers that the building of the human organism, including the brain, requires the presence of an intelligence who knows just how to accomplish the task and that this intelligence must pre-exist somewhere as something and must have gained its knowledge by experience in building, one is apt to conclude that this intelligence, or soul, is non-physical in nature, and that it is calling upon its memory of past experiences to aid in the construction of the human form. Therefore it is unlikely that any future physical theory will account for the memory trace, because in meeting the requirements of gaining knowledge through experience, the intelligence or soul must, of necessity, have an existence in non-physical substance and use non-physical energies.

Man's soul, residing in the finer substances we call astral and using the higher frequency-levels of the astral realm, embraces experiences with building necessary to construct the physical form and the totality of experience since it was brought into existence to fill a definite cosmic need for a given type of worker in the Divine Plan of Progressive Evolution. All experiences are retained as memory.

As academic psychologists become more and more interested in comprehensive analysis of ALL relevant factors connected with the human intelligence, so will more and more of them gain the courage to admit that past and present physical theories fall far short of explaining the human mind, conscious and unconscious. Such an admission will allow them to adopt the necessary theories of astral substance and astral frequencies in their efforts to clarify and explain human consciousness.

The courage and honesty to admit that a present theory is inadequate to explain phenomena is a necessary first step before formulating a different and more inclusive theory. In time, some of our physicists will realize and state in public that present theories offer little to explain the common phenomena associated with matter—such as solidity, form, opacity, transparency, etc.—and they will adopt the theory of astral energies and astral substance as essential to clarify the most common as well as the most complex behavior of physical matter.

As these steps are taken—and they will be in good time—the realization that the atheistic materialist does not have a genuine scientific leg to stand on will become more general. Then progress toward the wider recognition of the inclusive and cosmic nature of Deity will become more rapid. Along with this progress will come a growing recognition that Deity is a God of Law and Order, and that a definite and understandable set of laws governs everything from the evolution of consciousness and the existence of form to the attainment of spirituality. A study of God's Laws will show that they are not subject to change or whim, but that they go on and on through all eternity, to the realization of the Divine Plan of Eternal Progression.

Through progress and understanding, the old idea of a man-sized God subject to all human frailties will be supplanted with a better conception of the all-inclusive Creator—the God of all Cosmos, who rules through immutable laws which may be subject to misinterpretation but never to change.

As the consciousness of scientists unfold and become more inclusive, instruction given in our schools will gradually become more comprehensive. The genuine scientists among scholars will provide the light that will encourage aspiring students to reach beyond the dictated limitations and get some of the facts about life and existence. This will be possible when outworn and unworkable theories are discarded and replaced with new theories that adequately explain common phenomena, such as memory.

As the consciousness of the human race gradually evolves, intellectual integrity will become more common, and then more rapid progress will result, and the closer will mankind be to realizing the ideal of a brotherhood of man and a Fatherhood of God, so necessary to establish a firm and lasting peace on earth. This progress will come as the Aquarian Age advances and as the racial consciousness evolves.

While we may think that materialism is a deplorable viewpoint, we should at the same time recognize that science had to progress and provide a more adequate basis for our philosophical journeys into the realm of what is usually called metaphysics. Progress may seem slow, but the attainment is certain.

SELF-MASTERY AND ATTAINMENT

SELF MASTERY demands that one learn to use directed thinking and induced emotion in order to accomplish the building of spiritual qualities without waste of time and energy.

The dial of consciousness can be understood when it is realized that its pointer is the arrow of attention and that the energies of mind and emotion are building or tearing down in the area toward which the arrow is pointed.

These energies of mind and emotion are associated with pleasure or pain, called conditioning energy. We are constantly using these energies in building up spiritual qualities or the contrary, whether we are conscious of the process or not. These qualities we are building determine character, future events (both physical and non-physical) and destiny of the soul upon physical dissolution.

Much has been said and written about demonstration. We might define demonstration as using the energies of mind and emotion to attract desired things and conditions to ourselves. Let us be very clear about one important facet of demonstration. In the universe, it is impossible to get something for nothing, or to attempt to get something for nothing, without spiritually down-grading the soul as a direct result of the type of thinking and feeling necessary to such effort.

Everything must have a source, money included. Such money as we attract or demonstrate must come from someone else. If we do not hold the mental attitude that we are fully prepared to render adequate service to society for what we expect to get from that society, when we attempt to demonstrate money we are trying to use mental black-jackery to rob someone else. An astounding amount of this form of stealing is continuously being done through using the powers of the mind. Such demonstration, because of the mental attitude associated with it, is paid for in loss of spirituality. No one gets away with it.

In demonstration, there is a formula of four parts: (1) Formulation: deciding just what condition or asset is desired. (2) Visualization: Seeing the condition or asset as complete and attained. (3) Vitalization: giving the mental picture as much mental and emotional (desire) energy as is possible. (4) Realization: having complete faith that the desired end will be accomplished. This formula is applicable to healing at a distance, to the development of spiritual qualities, and to many other constructive uses.

Albeit unconsciously, it is often used to bring disaster to self, to friends and to family. For example: One's teenage children are out at night in a car with other teenagers. One starts to worry about them and decides they might be in a wreck or otherwise harmed *Formulation* has taken place. Worry builds to the extent that a mental picture of the children in a wreck or being harmed in some way is formed. *Visualization* has been accomplished. One becomes extremely upset emotionally, adding a great deal of energy to the picture. *Vitalization* part of the formula is fulfilled. In addition, having used all of the rest of the process of demonstration to build destructive forces up to this point, one feels very sure that the pictured condition is a reality. The conditions of *Realization* are met.

If the teenagers arrive home safely after this, it will be in spite of efforts to bring disaster to them through using all of the powers of mind and emotion to demonstrate catastrophe.

Of course, fear is the primary emotion at the beginning of what we call our period of worry. The above example shows the necessity of not only learning quite a lot about the mind and its powers but also the importance of learning how to use these powers constructively. Otherwise, that which we greatly fear will keep on coming to us, because we work so hard to demonstrate it into our lives. We do not intentionally do so, but we fulfill all of the four-part formula for demonstrating and must take the consequences.

It is far better to picture the children as enjoying themselves; feeling certain that they are very much all right, and that in due time they will return home safe and sound, and looking forward to their arrival with pleasure and love. This way we can help them be safe and sound. On the contrary, if we worry and work to bring disaster to them and if in spite of this, they get home safely, it does not seem very good religion, or even too sincere to blurt out, "Thank God! You're safe!"

In the individual case, a good idea is to hold a mental picture of one's self continually building a better channel through adding more and ever more spiritual qualities to one's soul. Of looking forward with pleasure to the opportunities presented by an ever-changing environment for such spiritual progress. And the picture of using these qualities as gained to assist the progressive evolution of mankind toward a progressively better civilization.

In order to get anything, we must find the means of getting it and of compensating cosmic society for the blessings expected and the blessings received. Part of the price we must pay for spiritual progress is learning how to use the mind and its powers for the benefit of self and the benefit of humanity as a whole.

Granted that up to the present time relatively few have learned to use those powers with a high degree of efficiency. Nonetheless, not only are these powers latent in every human being, but the ability to learn to use them with a very high degree of efficiency is also latent.

To effectively practice Mental Alchemy, Spiritual Alchemy and Cosmic Alchemy, one must of necessity understand the energies of the mind, the relationship of the individual to God and to cosmic society, for without understanding usefulness is impossible. In addition to understanding the energies of the mind, one must know how to use them constructively, and last but by no means least through directed thinking and induced emotion one must build an intense desire to work with God in the Divine Plan.

The arrow of attention should keep the consciousness tuned in as much as possible (with full consideration of physical needs) on the Creator and the Divine Plan, and on fitting oneself to be a better and better worker and partner in the fulfillment of Cosmic Needs.

The fact that each soul is brought into being to fulfill the need of Deity for a particular worker in the Divine Plan is something that should never be forgotten, even for one day. The thought that we are necessary to God is of vast importance to the aspiring souls. The fact that God is necessary to us and to Creation as a whole should help us to the realization that as part of Creation, we are co-existent, co-eternal and therefore should be cooperative with God.

Thus far, most of us have failed to take advantage of our opportunities and start to work to develop the powers of our minds and put them to use for our own benefit. Many of us have viewed this development as just a lot of hard work. And some, like one student we know, are just a bit afraid that they might have to give up something of value if they develop a spiritual consciousness. This student wanted all of the course on Mental Alchemy except the lesson entitled, Just How to Attain Realization. He was afraid that if he attained realization, he might have to give up some physical activity.

If we compared this attitude to that of an acorn that just did not want to become an oak tree because of the work involved, or because the acorn was afraid that in order to become an oak tree, it would have to give up its little hard shell; we might conclude that some prefer to be nuts throughout eternity, rather than grow into useful trees. The little hard shells of fear that some build about themselves are very effective in inhibiting growth; and so long as they are maintained, they act as a bar to intellectual and spiritual progress.

Some of us like to invent various escape mechanisms in order to avoid the necessity of facing ourselves as we really are and to try to avoid facing our responsibilities as part of Creation and the necessity of facing facts of our relationships to God and to society. If we have studied a little Astrology, we are quite likely to remark, "Well, Saturn is so and so, and I can't do it now." To which we reply, "Saturn equals the safety urges in the subconscious mind and labor and responsibility, among other things, and we do not know how you would get along without them, or without your skeleton, which Saturn also equals.

Others, like another friend we knew long, long ago, say, "I am going to study these things when I get time."

To him, we stated, "You have 24 hours in your day, no one who ever lived on earth has had any more or any less time. It is not the time you have, but what you do with that time that counts."

He admitted the accuracy of the statement.

Overcoming obstacles is the surest method of building the Will Power so essential to effective use of directed thinking and induced emotion in intellectual and spiritual progress. These obstacles (the squares of Astrology) actually afford the finest of opportunities to develop intellectual ability and a more spiritual character. It is an error to view any aspect as "bad."

The potentials of intellectual and spiritual growth latent in the human soul are literally as boundless as the Eternity of which the soul is an integral part. We can use the formula of demonstration, and we can use the arrow of attention on the dial of our individual consciousness to good advantage.

We need not go on and on, surrounded by a little hard shell of fear, afraid to grow and develop our potentials; for we can realize that we are One with God, and by keeping that fact ever before our attention, banish the little fears from our minds and live much more happy and much more useful lives.

We need not use the powers of the mind in a negative manner and continue to demonstrate everything we are sure we do not want. On the contrary, we can awaken the God within our individual consciousness and begin to demonstrate that which is most desirable of all human achievements—Unity with God and Conscious cooperation in the fulfillment of the Divine Plan.

Everyone is always standing at the Two Paths of Major Arcanum VI, (the sixth tarot card pictured in C. C. Zain's Sacred Tarot) deciding day by day which way to go, which way is the most desirable. When we have developed some of the latent powers of our consciousness and awakened to some of the realities of life; the choice is ever the constructive pathway. We study to learn, and we learn to study, so that our immense potentials may bring happiness, understanding and fully conscious union with God.

HABITS FOR ETERNAL PLEASURE

THE HUMAN being is a creature of habits. Various habits of thought, feeling and action equal the character as it exists at any moment of time. These habit-systems of reacting to stimuli determine whether or not the individual is a success or a failure in meeting the problems of every-day existence, and whether or not he is happy or sad.

If reacting in a certain way to a given type of stimulus—be it an astrological aspect or an environmental circumstance—produces a painful reaction, then it should be obvious that the way to obtain a pleasurable reaction is to displace the old way of thinking, feeling and acting in relation to this particular stimulus with a new habit-system.

If a given combination of factors "Makes one unhappy" because one thinks, feels and acts in a certain manner in relation to them, then a change of reaction is necessary. The method of thinking, feeling and acting should be changed so that a pleasurable feeling is experienced in relation to the same stimulus. Then it is correct to state that the same combination of factors now "makes one happy." Thus happiness or unhappiness does not consist of a combination of factors, a series of events, or a given type of stimulus. Happiness or the lack of it is the result of patterns of reaction built up through thinking, feeling and acting in relation to stimulus.

A new habit-system cannot be cultivated without displacing an old one. It is well, therefore to endeavor to replace old methods of reacting to stimuli with new methods that have a pleasurable reaction.

In traveling toward the goal of completely constructive thinking, feeling and acting, which brings happiness, working techniques must be developed. How to develop these techniques is set forth by C. C. Zain in his books *Esoteric Psychology, Personal Alchemy, Mental Alchemy, Spiritual Alchemy* and *Occultism Applied.*

The individual chart of birth and its progressions provide the Golden Key to the individual needs. Finding happiness lies in a combination of the individual chart and the practice of the techniques set forth in the above mentioned books.

One method that helps a very great deal in learning to live a completely constructive life is the habit-system of prayer. Grace before meals helps tune the consciousness (soul) in on spiritual realms and intelligences and assists in developing other constructive habit-systems.

In the art of practicing our religion, the late Elbert Benjamine has this to say: "The sincere member of The Church of Light has an eager desire to contribute his utmost to universal welfare. His effort to develop his own powers, and to acquire the facilities and securities of life, are not prompted merely by desire for self-gratification. On the contrary, they are understood by him to be aids by which he can more effectively assist in the realization of God's Great Plan.

"In the attention which he must give to the various more material interests, it is easy for him to become absorbed by them to the exclusion of his more comprehensive ideal. To prevent this, it is a commendable habit to call attention of the unconscious mind to the ideal striven for several times a day. Saying grace before each meal affords excellent opportunity for this.

"The cells of the food eaten have a consciousness of their own which also may be reached in this manner, and through the power of suggestion thus applied their activities within the system more effectively and harmoniously directed.

"Furthermore, whether man realizes it or not, he lives in an environment of inner-plane intelligences which are attracted, and to a degree influenced, by his thoughts. Saying grace, especially when performed in deep devotion, is a means of reaching harmoniously the intelligences of his inner-plane environment."

CHURCH OF LIGHT GRACE

"O Thou Eternal Spirit, in Whom we live, move, breathe and have our being! Consecrate this food we are about to partake of, to our bodies, to our souls, and to ministers of Thine who may be present, May peace be ever between us! So Shall It Be!"

The Church of Light Mantram, the Spiritual Texts of Astrology, and the Admonitions of The Sacred Tarot provide ample material for meditation to help the striving soul up the pathway of Spiritual Achievement. If used sincerely, until it becomes accepted as a fact by the soul, the following mantram will assist a great deal in furthering the desire to cultivate good habits of thought, feeling and action.

MANTRAM

"O Thou Eternal Spirit, in Whom we live, move, breathe and have our being! It is my desire that all of my thoughts, feelings and actions be directed by spiritual desire, in order that I might better function as a constructive part of the Divine Plan, and be of the utmost assistance in bringing to mankind an understanding of Thy Plan and Thy Divine Law. So Shall It Be!"

In moving an amount of material weighing several tons, one does not attempt to take it all in one armfull. If it must be moved by hand, the method to be followed is to take such loads as one can handle without becoming over tired or completely exhausted before the task is completed.

The habit-systems of thought, feeling and action that one has acquired up to any moment of time are a rather large amount of Soul Baggage. In order to replace the old with the desired new, it is necessary to take them one at a time so that the task can be accomplished. If one tried to change them all at once, failure is bound to result, because more mental exertion is called for than one is capable of putting forth at any given time. There are too many tons (so to speak) of material to move all at once.

Speaking to an inhabitant of earth, a Spiritual Master said, "You folks don't know anything about patience." Yet patience is necessary to developing constructive habit-systems, because it keeps one at the task. Will power is needed, too, because it is a life long task.

It is rather difficult for we Earthlings to realize the tremendous patience required to build and direct the functions of a solar system or a universe, yet this work is done by servants of the Divine One we call God.

Billions and trillions of earth years are involved, yet the great work must be done according to plan and under Divine Law. That is patience. When impatience rears its head, this thought will stay the restlessness that is a companion to impatience.

When one has done his best, even if the desired results have not been obtained, the habit of feeling satisfied with the effort needs to be cultivated. Such feelings are necessary to combat the feelings of discouragement which add energy to the discordant mental elements, providing more material that must be moved in order to accomplish the desired result.

Sincere effort is never lost. Knowledge can be gained from the experience and a better technique developed. This is progress.

Each circumstance of life presents a problem that has a best possible solution. In changing old habit-systems for new and better habit-systems, a problem is involved. Viewing each circumstance as a problem and developing a pleasurable attitude in the task of finding its solution is the best approach. This is called *the problem attitude and the pleasure technique.*

Such an attitude enables one to recondition the thought cells of the soul (subconscious mind) toward a continually more pleasurable response, and assists one in becoming more happy and more useful day by day.

Of course, there will be obstacles in the way. Astrologically, obstacles are mapped as square aspects. Every stairway presents an obstacle. One must overcome the inertia of his own weight and exert sufficient muscular power to raise that weight from a lower to a higher level in order to climb the stairs. When this has been accomplished, that particular obstacle is overcome.

A trine aspect in a chart is usually called fortunate, because those things it represents are supposed to come without effort. Yet, without effort, progress is not possible. The difference between a trine and a square was well summed up in an astrological student's comment: "There is an apple in a tree. Under the trine aspect, you walk under the tree and the apple falls into your hands. Under a square, the apple is still there, but you must climb the tree in order to get it."

One may well learn to enjoy the effort necessary to get the apple and to enjoy the apple all the more because of the feeling of achievement associated with it. That is, a problem is presented, a technique is used, an obstacle overcome, and pleasure obtained.

The conditions represented by the so-called *bad aspects* in a horoscope provide the greatest opportunities to develop strength through overcoming obstacles. These aspects are called the square, semi-square, sesqui-square and opposition. Without the obstacle—representing a resistance of environment to an action—it is impossible to make progress. Only through overcoming, may one partake of the hidden manna of Conscious Spiritual Progress. And only by overcoming obstacles may old habit-systems of a destructive nature be displaced with new ones that "make one happy."

What the so-called bad aspects do represent is the painful conditioning energy that has been added to the thought cells of the basic urges as mapped by the planets. When this painful conditioning energy has been replaced with pleasurable conditioning energy, through the cultivation of new and constructive habit systems of thinking, feeling and acting in relation to the stimuli of progression in the horoscope or circumstances in the environment, one no longer responds in the old manner.

As a consequence, character and destiny have been changed. Thus, each soul has in its possession the potential of altering the meaning of the individual birth chart to the extent that it no longer means what it once did.

Because each person must think, feel, and act for self, each is responsible for the individual progress or lack of it, as the case may be. Because one cannot think, feel and act for another, one should cultivate the habit of viewing each person—no matter in what relationship—as an independent soul working out its own destiny, a minute but essential part of the Divine Plan.

Such a habit allows the ultimate development of the virtue of understanding, a necessity for continued progress. It also helps displace the habit of trying to control the thoughts and feelings of others, which is, in essence trying to play God (a role for which no mortal is fitted). Thus it is a step on the way to attaining Cosmic Mindedness.

Seeing self and others in relation to society as a whole and to the Divine Plan is an essential attribute to Cosmic Mindedness. When a correct perspective is attained, it helps to overcome the bad habit of egotism by substituting a good habit of seeing correct relationships.

When one perceives self in cosmic perspective, one is in better position to evaluate the problem of soul progression and to apply the priceless pleasure-technique to its solution.

Good habit-systems of thought and feeling enable one to get along with the population of the earth in a harmonious manner to a much larger extent than otherwise would be possible.

A very simple test of the relative values can be had in any community of a hundred or so people. On one test day, start out with a frown and give short terse answers to questions, be cross and growl at people as do those folk who have that sort of habit-system.

On the next test day, start out with a smile, find time for a cheery word and greeting to others, act as pleasant as possible. At the end of each day, take note of other people's reactions and your own feelings. The result should provide ample proof of the benefits of the good habit-system with its attendant pleasure technique.

It is not a sacrifice to exchange something of little value for something of great value. Such an exchange is usually called good business. Trading habit-systems of thought, feeling and action which produce pain, discouragement and sadness in general for habit-systems that lead to gaining "the peace that passeth understanding" is good spiritual business. The happiness gained is worth vastly more than the old reaction.

Under the Divine Plan, the bargain counter where bad habit-systems may be exchanged for good ones is always open. The price one pays is the development of potentials. Everyone has potentials. They are a free will gift of God.

There is always a sign on the door which can be read by all who desire to enter: "Spiritual rewards are yours for the taking. Leave all discordant thoughts and feelings outside. The road you see leads to your spiritual home."

When one desires peace in the home or neighborhood, his problem is to establish a set of harmonious relations between the people involved. If there has been discord, one or more persons must change the habit-system of reacting in order to bring harmony. If all persons really want harmony, it can come through the exchange of old habit-systems for new. There is nothing impossible about the problem. The same factors apply to nations.

Peace on earth is nothing more or less than a set of harmonious relationships between individuals and groups of people. Peace is brought about by cultivating good habit-systems of thought, feeling and action through the establishment of harmony in the place of prevalent discord. It cannot be obtained in any other manner.

When one person is determined that harmony shall not exist when two people are involved, it will not exist so far as that one person is concerned. But that does not prevent the other from trading old systems of reacting for new and obtaining peace within.

Where nations are concerned, harmonious relationships (peace) can exist whenever the leader of any two desire it. When the leaders of all the nations of the world are willing to recognize what peace is and sincerely work to establish the necessary harmony, we shall have achieved a real basis for beating swords into ploughshares.

In the individual case, each can work for peace through cultivating and using good habits of thought, feeling and action. When enough people do this, peace on earth and good will among all mankind will follow.

It is useless for the individual to pray to God to do something for him which he is unwilling to do for himself. God has freely given him the means to do it. In the international sense, it is useless to try to get God to force a set of good habit-systems of thought, feeling and action upon some would-be or actual Dictator who does not want them. There is only one way for the individual to obtain peace within, just as there is only one way for peoples or nations to be at peace with each other.

Through a bountiful God, the means of attaining peace are always at hand. Whether they are used or not is up to the individual, the group, or the nations.

The bargain counter is always open, the prices never change, the values remain constant. Peace on earth or in the individual soul can be had for the taking, providing one is willing to give up a set of bad habit-systems that produce painful reactions for good habits that yield eternal pleasure.

MORAL CONCEPTS

IN MOST regions of the earth, what is believed to be moral and right is what some religious leader has dictated to the followers of the particular religion should be considered moral and right.

The moral concepts of the Pilgrim fathers, for instance, did not extend to their dealings with the Indians. One must be honest with one's own kind, but it was moral to lie to and cheat the Indians.

The moral concepts of those who conducted the Inquisition allowed them to inflict unbelievable tortures upon those who held differing beliefs in order to convert them to a particular religion.

The moral concepts of the Hindu allowed for the marriage of female children to old men but did not allow one to kill a wounded cow to end her suffering.

Whatever the moral concepts of a particular group and no matter how these concepts may differ from those of other groups, each one of them is convinced that they are right, and furthermore that these concepts are Divinely Inspired.

And each group is certain that God has ordered reward for adhering to its own moral code and punishment of one sort or another for disobeying the moral code.

That there might be a Universal Moral Code and a Universal Law of Soul Progression, decreed and administered by a God of Law and Order is not considered. It is not considered, because this idea would—if adopted—place all of Creation, including all of life, all souls, all morals upon a single immutable basis and completely do away with the egotistical attempts to dictate to God, what God should do.

Given the idea of a Universal Moral Code—with its corrollary of what is right for one is right for all, whether one is considering individuals or nations—mankind would evolve much faster toward the desired Peace on Earth and Good Will among Mankind than is possible with the many moral concepts and many ideas of a God of human frailties and a God of special privilege as presently envisioned by so many of the human race.

Most of the moral codes of mankind, whether they be those that allow torture of heretics, child marriage, the eating or not eating of pork, the stealing of the lands of differing peoples, headhunting, murder, rape, slavery, few clothes or many, have been throughout the ages and are to this day believed to be Divinely Ordained by those who follow them.

To put it bluntly, these are tribal concepts of morals similar to the morals of a mother hen toward her own chickens, and the morals of the same hen to other broods. Let a bird in a flock start to behaving differently than his fellows—whether because of sickness or for some other reason—and more often than not, he is killed or segregated.

Even today, let some member of the human race believe and behave differently than his fellows, within an area limited to some particular religious group, the persecution is very apt to be similar to that of the flock of birds toward the fellow who is different.

These practices arise from the moral concepts of the group and are firmly believed to be moral and right by that group.

The leader who dictated the moral code may be completely ignorant of what God does, as evidenced by the operations of God in his own garden or for that matter in his own body. Yet that leader is quite certain that he is the final authority as to what God wants in relation to moral concepts and that he (the leader) knows all about Divine Law.

The idea of a Universal Moral Code such as: "A soul is completely moral when it is contributing its utmost to Universal Welfare" does not and cannot occur to the mind that has not investigated what God does in order to determine what God wants. There is a Universal Law of Soul Progression and a Universal Law of Compensation that go hand in hand with the Universal Moral Code.

To discuss these laws in detail is not the function of this brief discourse. Here the attempt is made to call the individual attention to these laws and to point out that a detailed discussion of these factors and the material upon which they are based may be found in the book entitled *"Organic Alchemy"* by C. C. Zain.

Each soul is an independent entity working out its own salvation, is the idea embraced by The Religion of The Stars, as is the Universal Moral Code and the Laws of Soul Progression and Compensation.

We believe that each soul must learn to accept the responsibility for its own progress, and that in so-doing starts to travel the highway toward Divine Consciousness.

SECURITY UNDER GOD'S LAW

THE GREAT 200-inch telescope at Mount Palomar has revealed the continuity of the same things that smaller telescopes have revealed. But a multitude of stars have been reported that were not seen before, and there is no evidence of any end or any beginning to the manifestation of the universe that we call God's Kingdom. Nor is there any evidence to indicate any beginning or ending to the manifestation we call life, to the manifestation which expresses as intelligence—directing the building of forms and directing the motions of those forms.

To attempt to find a beginning or ending of life is quite as futile as man's attempt to find a beginning or ending to the starry heavens with any instrument he possesses or can conceivably manufacture.

Each human individual is a part of the divine expression called life. He is not separate nor distinct from it, except as he is an individualized mode of motion within that divine whole called life.

Because of the universal educational factors of pleasure and pain, the human individual concludes that so-and-so to which he reacts painfully is bad or very bad, depending upon the degree of pain; and that to which he reacts pleasurably is good or very good, depending upon the degree of pleasurable emotion with which his responses have been conditioned to the particular kind of stimuli.

Yet if we start to examine the evolution of intelligence—the evolution of a soul—it does not take very long for us to ascertain that without experiences called bad or painful, the soul would not evolve at all. Perhaps this is so of all which is called bad or painful.

Any person who has reached the point where he truly desires to know why he is on earth, what his mission in life is, what he is supposed to do about it, and undergoes the soul-searching which is necessary to find out the truth of the matter, will invariably come to the conclusion that without his particular set of experiences—those called bad in particular—he could not have arrived at the point of desiring to know the truth about his soul, his Universe, his God.

We see a multitude of discords upon the face of the earth in the form of wars. We see other multitudes of discord in the shape of religious disagreements. We see numerous groups almost without number who desire in one form or another to control the thoughts and feelings of other groups of people. If we were capable—and we are not—of determining the truth about what is desired of life upon earth by the Being we call God, we would find out that all of those apparent discords are necessary to the evolutionary process of life upon earth. They play an important role in educating the human race as a whole and in assisting the race to fulfill its divine destiny.

Following the pleasure and pain conditioning techniques in the evolutionary process of religions, man has invented everything from a burning hell to glaciers in the midst of fire, to which he is going to confine those souls after death who disagree with his particular religious concepts. He has also invented a devil with a forked tail and cloven hoofs, one who wields a vicious weapon.

On the other side, man has invented a man-sized God with all the human frailties. A God who becomes angry at His own creations and condemns to hell-fire and damnation all of the souls that do not turn out as He wanted them to in the first place. This is a lot of poppy-cock, as there is only one creator who knows exactly what He is doing.

If intelligence is the adaptation of the exigencies of life as they actually exist in the infinitude called God, Who embraces all that is, has been, or ever can be—motion, substance, intelligence, limitless time and space—then these man-made theories will not stand up. This is so for a simple reason. Man does not know it all. Substance embraces infinite degrees, those discerned by man's feeble instruments and those as yet unseen. The energy which makes all, moves all, does all, is the energy of God expressing as life.

We, as part of that divine whole, cannot well take the position of condemning some part of life as *bad*, unless we are also willing to take the position of condemning the Creator of that life. For in condemning the work of an individual, we also condemn that individual. Therefore, unless we are willing to honestly within our own soul call God a bungler—a being who does not know what he is doing, a being in Whom no dependence can be placed (to obey our order!)—we had better come to the conclusion that the manifestation we call life is *good*, all of it. The manifestation we call God is not making any mistakes. Such limitations as there may be are limitations within the individual's consciousness which keeps him from beholding at the time the entirety of the matter; thus, the truth of the matter.

If a little child were shown one of the photos taken through the Palomar telescope, he would not understand it. The starry heavens are revealed as pin-points of light. This little child could hardly be expected to stretch his mind over the vastness of space covered by the photo, to say nothing of comprehending what a *light year* is. You could tell him that a certain star was so many light years from the earth, but he would not grasp your statement. Then later in explaining the measurements of the astronomers which run up to 6 trillions of miles multiplied by 3 or 4 or 5 hundred times, and even more for the distances to the outer galaxies, your words would convey no meaning at all to him.

As the child's mind has not been trained to grasp the expansion of a concept from a small photo to the expanse of the heavens, the picture would not mean any more to him than a bunch of light bulbs photographed in a large room. True, that is the only meaning of the photo for a number of adults also.

If the child has trouble—and we are much more infantile in our comprehension of the manifestation called life than the little child is in comprehending the meaning of the Palomar photographs of the heavens—don't you think it is just a little bit egotistical to take it upon ourselves to condemn some part of God's creation?

After all, all the creation we can see manifests on an infinitestimal, relatively speaking, speck of dust in the universe called earth. Don't you think man is egotistical in his condemnation when the entirety of life, even with the 200-inch telescope, is far beyond his ability to take in even as points of dim light?

It pays to be a little bit cautious in evaluating this process called life, especially its goodness or badness. Furthermore, so far as the practical adaptation to the problems of everyday living is concerned, we become much more happy people if we conclude that all of God's manifestation is *good* and he did not make any mistakes, that there must be some reason for what seems bad even though we do not understand it.

Instead of condemning, we could save ourselves a great deal of emotional disturbance by looking at things around us, by trying to learn from them. The evolution of the child's mind from the point where he sees only white spots on a piece of paper (those dim distant stars) to the point where a mind can visualize a constellation, a galaxy, or a universe similar to our own is quite a long process of development.

As a matter of fact, the child has to go to school; he has to study; he has to learn something insofar as his teachers and textbooks are capable of imparting information or misinformation to him. True, he has to learn, but he does not do it in fifteen minutes. He might get down on his knees and pray for understanding, but if he doesn't make any effort on his own part he will never learn. Under the law, no *one* of the individual expressions of life ever gets something for nothing.

In short, nothing is done or created without an expenditure of energy. Nothing comes to a person that belongs to him alone unless he has expended some energy to get it. In the process of developing the understanding to find the relationship between self and God, one has to expend a very considerable amount of effort. And he must pay the inescapable price of being absolutely sincere in his search.

There is no power on the face of the earth or off of it that can stop the individual who knocks upon the door correctly from having that door opened to him. It is not within the bounds of human power to stop, stay, or change the constantly "going on" evolutionary processes of life that are supposedly designed to fulfill some divine purpose. Just what, we do not always know.

It is within the power of each individual to choose whether or not he is going to become a sincere person without unduly punishing himself, to choose whether or not he is going to continue to bring pain to himself down to the fact that we can make our lives miserable or happy by the dominant attitude we hold.

Just as the planets do not have the power to get out of their orbits, and just as our vaunted power of the atom bomb is no complete protection, we cannot change the rotation of the earth or alter a single thing in our own little solar system.

Nor can all of the earthly weeping and wailing cause the star Sirius to move closer to or further from the earth, or get out of its orbit. So also does no single soul have the power to become something different than what the Creator designed it to be in the first place. A soul does have the power of free will choice in selecting the easy way or the hard way of life. That is the limit of free will.

Would it not be awful if a handful of little human beings could upset the whole divine purpose of all of this vast system of universes that we see stretching out before our goggled eyes into an ever greater infinitude of space? That would be something, wouldn't it?

All that we can see or imagine, all that we consider life has substance and energy in action on a definite level of existence, and is contained within the one divine whole. We, as parts of the whole, are individualized modes of motion. In one sense, we are parts of the evolutionary process of life. And in another sense, we are individuals evolving to develop and use an intelligent free will in cooperating with the divine whole to fulfill a mission.

If we do not choose at any time to strive to find our divine cause for being, to find our place in the divine scheme, then we are not quite ready yet and other things will seem more pleasurable. That attitude in itself does not condemn a soul to any hell, except the hell of emotional discords of his own making through ignorance. Nor does God get mad because He made a botch of that part of creation!

Such an attitude means that the soul has not yet evolved intelligence enough to know how it can exercise free will to attract pleasure to itself. No soul within the divine whole ever finds the real meaning of pleasure until it unites itself with God in the divine purpose of eternal evolution. Until a soul finds his relationship with God, his place in the divine plan, his *reason d'etre,* he will continually undergo emotional upsets of one sort or another. We do not attract security until we understand the law, consciously or unconsciously.

Until we become independent thinkers, we blame he, she or it for the things which happen to us. That "it" takes in a lot of territory—a neighbor, dog, door, or what have you. In so doing, we allot to the he, she or it the power of dictation over our own emotional responses. Such reasoning is erroneous as we do the responding ourselves. No one outside of ourselves thinks, feels and acts for us.

Therefore, we make ourselves what we are. "As a man thinketh so is he." We determine what we shall be, and we go about being what we *will* to be or *will* to make ourselves at any given time.

Whether or not our decisions will bring us pleasure depends upon the intelligence or lack of it with which we fashion our characters. What God *does not* do is force us to be something that we do not want to be. What God *does* do is provide the educational system which—in the long run—will make us be what He wants us to be.

God's laws operate night and day, without pausing for one instance, without ever a hesitation. They are much more simpler than most people think they are. The laws govern changes produced in the substance of the soul under the impact of energy—the energy of our mind and emotions.

That is what makes our characters, what makes ourselves, and what makes our destinies.

Cogitations on the manifestation of life result in a great respect and a deep affection for the Being we call God. There is no other possible method under the sun by which souls could be treated absolutely fairly than under the security of God's law.

We need not depend upon the edict of some particular religion, posing as a law of God, but we can depend upon the operation of unchanging law, under which all changes are brought about in the innumerable types of substance. God's laws are as understandable as a simple fulcrum. There is no mystery. A human mind can grasp the principles. Then the knowledge of what a particular thought or emotion does to a particular soul comes with exactness. How thought and emotion affect life here and hereafter. That is of value, because it allows us to select our thoughts and emotions with much more care than we otherwise would.

Most people sit down to the table of life's fare and take anything that comes along without ever determining whether or not an emotional response is good. If a discordant reaction comes about, most of them will be heard to say, "Anyway, it wasn't my fault. It was somebody over there at the other end of the table. He is to blame."

Somebody at the other end of the table could not possibly think and feel for the individual. Let us, as one of the first steps, accept self-responsibility for self thoughts and self feelings. Let us try to make ourselves into the kind of being that we think we ought to be. And for sure, into the kind of being that desires to understand his relationship to God. Let us resolve to cooperate with the divine plan of perpetual evolution, intelligently fulfilling our particular place and evolving on as ability increases towards new and greater responsibilities.

A good and busy place, this universe is always in motion. There is no such thing within it as a cessation of motion. The human soul either moves ahead spiritually, or it retrogresses for a time. It is never lost. It does not and cannot stand still. The apparent retrograde motion of a soul results from its lowering its basic character vibratory rate through discordant thoughts and feelings.

But once the law is understood, there is no excuse for retrogression. God's plan operates under divine law. The security of a soul is safe under that law. God does not play favorites, so it is placed in our own hands to make our lives happy or unhappy. All souls are treated just alike, regardless of their religious convictions, color, creed, or stage of evolution. The law is impersonal and immutable.

You can engender a profound respect and place an abiding faith in that kind of God. You can go ahead and face the tomorrows of life, completely unafraid for you know you have security under His law.

LOVE IS NOT FOR SALE

EVERYONE wants to be loved and cherished. Perhaps you have said, "I would give anything if I could only have a happy marriage!" If so, it is time to do a little thinking and come to a few realizations regarding you, the other person and the much-to-be-desired love.

"Love is never retained by force, nor by complaining, nor by finding fault, nor by any other disagreeable activity. It is either held through the exercise of lovable qualities or it is lost." C. C. Zain.

In the spiritual sense, husbands, wives, relatives and friends are all independent souls working out their own destinies. They do not belong to us any more than our physical bodies belong to us. In each case, they are associated with us during physical existence, and we may or may not reunite with them when we and they pass on to a new life in astral or spiritual worlds, depending upon individual attainments.

Love of one person for another can only be gained and retained through kindness, consideration and an unselfish desire to see the other person happy. True, the other person must also desire to love and exercise the same consideration in return if we are to achieve a completely satisfying affectional relationship. It is only thus that the ideal of each contributing to the physical, intellectual and spiritual welfare of the other can be attained—the real purpose of marriage.

Being human and constantly evolving toward the goal of perfection, people—including husbands and wives—make mistakes. It is proper to recognize an error and find means of correcting the attitude and actions to prevent its repetition. It is not proper to find fault, criticize and indulge in self-pity over the error which may have been made. Remember, love is not for sale. It can be attained and kept only by exercising lovable qualities. Intelligent understanding demands the recognition of the facts of life and love.

When we were a half century younger, we used to have a task of milking several cows, night and morning. Cows, like people, are subject to changing moods. Once in a while a cow, feeling peevish, would set a foot right in the middle of the milk pail, then kick. A gallon or so would spill on the ground. We never tried to pick up the spilled milk. We knew that was useless. Nor have we ever seen a cat so foolish as to try to dig after milk soaking into the ground; cats have too much sense!

Crying over spilled milk or some error does not help matters. What can be done is to learn from the experience and ascertain how to avoid the same mistake. If we desire to retain love, wailing over what is past will solve nothing. On the contrary such foolish action does add energy to the discord and assists in killing the affection the other person may have felt for us.

If we are sincere in our desire to gain a better understanding and retain or gain a higher degree of affection for the other person, obviously we will be forced to be a loving, understanding, kind and considerate person ourselves.

All of the gold buried in Fort Knox cannot purchase one iota of genuine love. Nor would a person possessing all of the gold and precious stones in the world be more lovable because of material possession. Conversely, a person possessing only a cotton sheet with which to clothe himself might—because of his quality of mind and emotion—be as lovable as it is humanly possible to be. It is not what is outside that counts. It is what is in the mind and soul that determines attitudes and reactions to events and conditions of environment.

To win love, one must give it. The great attractive force in nature is love. It is symbolically pictured at the center of the Tree of Life in the Sacred Tarot. In Spiritual Alchemy, it is pictured as the reverberatory furnace where the metals (attitudes) of life are transmuted into Spiritual Gold. Love must be unselfish, kind, considerate, trustworthy and trusting in order to be spiritual.

Of course, there are grades and degrees of love, because all attraction from atomic to angelic is a form and a degree of love. The souls of men and women who fail to exercise the qualities necessary to gain and retain a high type of unselfish affection are ever restless, ever unsatisfied, ever yearning for something different—something that the individual, rightly or wrongly, considers better.

God is Love, and Life and Light are expressions of Love. Love—like spirituality, intelligent understanding, kindness and consideration—is not for sale for any physical consideration. The formula for love is Know Yourself, Be Yourself and Give Yourself in loving consideration for the well being of others.

THE ANCIENT ALCHEMISTS

IN THIS more or less enlightened age we are prone to view those of the past as being intellectually and spiritually inferior to ourselves. Thus our egotistic urges ever tend to make us just a wee bit swell headed.

Modern science has laughed at the ancient forerunners of chemistry et al, in their supposed efforts to transmute physical base metals into the more alluring and enduring gold. It is entirely true that, by many, this was the end sought. Even in this, science is rapidly discovering that those old boys were not quite so crazy as they at first seemed, for transmutation of one metal into another is now commonly recognized as a possibility through changing the atomic weights of the component parts.

But there was yet another ancient alchemist, apparently utilizing the same means and same symbols as those who sought so mightily in the effort to make physical gold. This branch sought to transmute the experiences of everyday life into spiritual values, which they called pure gold.

In this search, in order to protect their lives from the current murderers who hid under the cloak of religion, they allied the groups of experiences of life to the various metals, and again to various planets which they thought expressed the same qualities as the experiences and metals allied to them.

Thus experiences with political power were allied to gold, and to the Sun. Experiences with domestic life and its relationship were allied to silver and the Moon. Those with intellectual pursuits to quicksilver and Mercury. Those with construction and destruction, warfare, etc., to iron and Mars. Those with benevolence to Jupiter and tin. And those with poverty, labor and responsibility, to lead and Saturn.

By utilizing these symbols, they were enabled to converse in a language that was unintelligible to the uninitiated.

They were thus enabled to pursue their search for the universal solvent of experiences in a comparative degree of safety. Seeking the means in the laboratory of life, by which they might ally themselves closer to the Creator of all things, they came to the conclusion, as their writings so clearly reveal to all who understand universal symbology, that Love was the common denominator that enabled the transmutation of the experiences of everyday life into eternal spiritual gold.

When one of them decided that he had not had quite enough lead Saturn, or sorrow to enable him to make the transmutation, this type of experience was deliberately sought out, and if some other type of experience was deemed necessary, this too was sought out. The only value attached to any of them was the effect upon the Soul of man, its appearance being regarded as an illusion, and that which they viewed as permanent value sought out.

Thus to them an experience or thing was neither good nor bad in itself. It became either only as a mental attitude was taken toward it. The mental and emotional response was viewed as the real underlying value; for this is what was thought to affect the soul and hasten or retard its progression in the Cosmic Scheme of things.

By viewing each experience in this manner, it became a very different thing than when looked at from the physical standpoint. The common method is to view each experience as it affects our physical pocketbooks and what we are pleased to call our physical well-being.

Love of fellowman, love of God, ever seeking to advance their souls and comprehension so that they might better serve as constructive parts of what they called The Divine Plan: these were the ends sought in the transmutation of the metals or experiences of life into pure gold or spiritual values.

Forced, they were, indeed to conceal the true nature of their search, beneath symbolism which had an inner meaning to themselves. Thus they sought to cultivate the soul and assist in its growth and expansion by working with natural laws; very much as a successful farmer plants, cultivates and reaps the harvest of his labors by assisting nature.

Perusing the foregoing the reader can perhaps see that these were also not quite so crazy as the appearance of their works would suggest.

Perhaps we, in our modern civilization might also learn something from them, if we can lay aside for a time the viewpoint that we are so much farther advanced and so much more civilized than were those ancient alchemists.

AQUARIAN AGE PHILOSOPHY

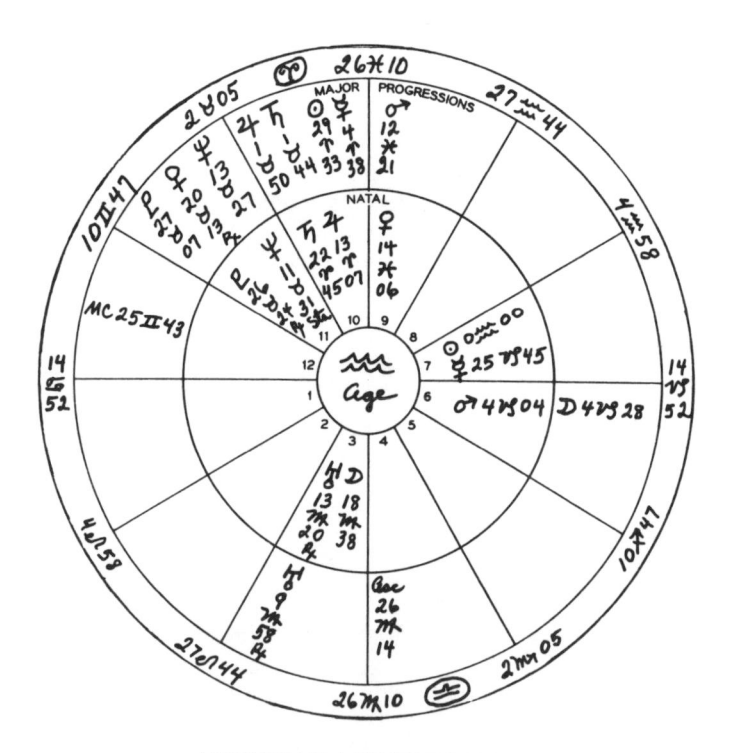

AQUARIAN AGE HOROSCOPE

January 19, 1881   3:48:24 P.M. Local Mean Time
Washington, D.C.   38N53 77W01   Sidereal Time 23h 45m 56s
Limiting Date, September 5, 1880. Progressed to 1970.

This Aquarian Age Chart maps the planetary energies available for now and in the future. To achieve success, the obstacles indicated must be surmounted to attract the Brotherhood of Man.

Astrology and Extrasensory Perception

III.

ASTROLOGY: ART OR SCIENCE

THROUGHOUT recorded history, those who would enslave the minds of men have attempted to keep them in ignorance to implant prejudice, and to inflame men into actions designed to put some dictator into power or to keep those in power who had already attained it. The propaganda techniques used appeal to the Drive for Significance, the Drive for Self Preservation and the Drive for Race Preservation. As promised benefits never materialize, this necessitates keeping the attention directed toward something other than a factual analysis of the situation as it is.

Ignorance plus prejudice equals bigotry.

As a rule, we do not take much notice of attacks upon astrology, because most of them are not worth attention. But if we did not remember the excuses and propaganda techniques used to destroy the Alexandrian Library and to burn the records of the Aztecs and Mayans, we should be derelict in our duty. In the case of the Aztecs, those suspected of possessing historical or astrological knowledge were executed.

When the article referred to in the following letter appeared in Redbook Magazine, we thought it our duty to take some action, because of the extreme prejudice and the abysmal ignorance displayed. And because of the effort to appeal to the Hereditary Drive for Self Preservation through attempting to implant the fear of loss of station and honor (the Drive for Significance) if one believed in astrology, even though one had spent years of time and much mental effort in proving it to himself. The suggestive device used here is emotional retardation. That is, everyone who believes in astrology, no matter why, so it implies is emotionally retarded. The letter follows.

The Editor
REDBOOK
230 Park Avenue
New York 17, New York

March 28, 1953

Dear Sir:

In the April 1953 issue of Redbook appears an article entitled, "Don't Believe Astrologers."

Up to the present time, we have assumed that in order to gain knowledge of anything, it was necessary to study the subject in question, subject it to the test of critical analysis and base whatever conclusions were arrived at on the evidence obtained.

However, in the article in question, the investigator posing as an authority must use different methods since according to his statements, he is unaware of the difference between Signs of the Zodiac and Mundane Houses. But nonetheless he feels amply qualified to state that it is difficult to explain what astrologers mean by astrology.

We submit in his case, it is not only difficult but impossible to explain something of which he so obviously knows nothing.

Yet, while in ignorance of the subject, he makes the assertion that it is an ancient fraud.

According to our experience, obtaining knowledge of anything requires that some process must be followed. That is, if knowledge is obtained, it must be obtained by some method. Obviously the method is not one of study of the subject and the use of time honored laboratory methods, but of necessity be something else. That something else to be anything, must be a method and have some plan of operation. We believe it is fair to ask just what that method is and how it operates.

In the case of the lady astrologer (unnamed) who is supposed to have so many clients, we note that no effort was made to check on the case histories and determine whether or not the claims were true. On the contrary, it was assumed (apparently) that irreparable harm was being done to these people by a person who seemed sincere. But because the person did not lay claims to certain qualifications, that she suffered from emotional retardation, was intellectually inferior to the investigator and star crazy or otherwise off the beam.

All of this was apparently determined by an assumed psychic ability since the usual methods of investigation were so completely disregarded. Not being content with using the propaganda techniques rendered so familiar by Radio Moscow on the astrologers alone, Wall Street Bankers who may use astrology because their experience has proven it a valuable asset are labeled as suckers, and it is intimated that they are emotionally retarded like the rest of us so-called star crazy people.

If a Wall Street Banker were so foolish as pictured, he would soon be on Skid Row instead of remaining a successful banker. It appears to us that this is the most remarkable assumption of all and requires the ability to make a psychiatric examination without knowing the person involved, the ability to read minds without knowing which one is being read, and to obtain a quite large mass of information this way. We do not believe that either the Editor or the investigator possesses the assumed knowledge or ability.

At this point we label the statement that astrology is an ancient fraud as completely false.

We teach astrology. We do not recommend astrologers or practice professional astrology. No one connected with our organization receives any pay for teaching. The reason we teach astrology is because it offers the best possible means of determining the mental and emotional equipment one possesses at birth, and aside from physical environment the type and relative volume of mental and emotional stimulation one is to receive at any time in the future. This enables one to use astrology to correct faulty habit systems of reaction and to plan the reconditioning of response to stimuli before the stimuli occurs. We regard astrology as one of the most valuable tools and cornerstones of our Religion. It is for that reason that we look upon this article as an attack—an attack without validity upon one of the cornerstones of our Religion.

It is stated that the Conception chart was devised by an English astrologer, and that it wasn't until last year that American astrologers came up with the solution, etc. We refer to Brotherhood of Light Lesson No. 117, copyright (USA) 1934, in which the method of determining the Conception chart is set forth under the heading Prenatal Epoch.

It is obvious that something is being twisted. We think the question is in order: Just who is twisting what?

A number of years ago, we desired to investigate certain claims of astronomers relative to determining stellar distances (parallax) by trigonometrical methods. It became necessary to trace the idea back to a lecture before the Royal Astronomical Society given by Sir John Herschel (Story of The Heavens, by Ball). We, then, obtained the best and most scientific text books in existence on astronomy, recommended to us by a number of leading astronomers. We spent some three years in rather intensive research before we came to certain conclusions. These conclusions were not too complimentary to the claims of distance determination. As part of the results, we will quote from the letter of one instructor in astronomy: "You have gone into the problem more thoroughly than I ever have." The evidence is documented along with a lot more.

In order to investigate, we thought it necessary to do some very intensive study of the subject. We did not assume that we could ascertain the facts without study, nor did we assume that we had any ability to explain until we had considerable knowledge of the subject. That is, we did not think that invective was a good substitute for investigation in the case of astronomy. And we do not think that assumption to knowledge obtained without study and which does not exist is a good substitute in the case of Astrology. In short, we do not believe that either the Editor or the so-called investigator possesses the remarkable powers that are here assumed.

Now it may be that your so-called investigator has investigated a few Astrologers. No documentation is presented. As to any claims made that he investigated Astrology, we must—on the evidence submitted in the article in question—state flatly that such claims are baseless and without foundation in fact.

So far as we are aware, this so-called investigation represents the first time Sincerity has been offered as evidence of a lack of emotional development. We are well aware that it is fashionable in certain academic circles to teach prejudice against astrology. We are further aware that the state of knowledge relative to the subject of astrology is conspicuous by its absence.

We do not believe that having a set of prejudices against something of which one knows nothing is any evidence of intellectual superiority, emotional development, or moral responsibility. We do not believe that assumption (in one's mind) of a superiority that does not exist, of knowledge that is not present, or psychic powers that are not present indicate qualifications for investigation of anything. On the contrary, it is our experience that such assumptions indicate factors best unearthed by a psychiatric examination and best named by the psychiatrist.

There is an old saying relative to study: "Crafty men condemn it, simple men admire it, wise men use it."

We do not mind being in error. It is our policy, and has been our policy, that when research disproves views previously held, to alter our views to conform to facts. We do not pretend to have complete knowledge of anything, including Astrology. But we firmly believe that the way to gain a more complete knowledge of anything is to keep on studying. This we have done and will continue to do so.

We insist that it is our right, when someone levels a stream of criticism at astrology—one of the cornerstones of our Religion—to demand that we be told precisely where we are in error and why we are in error. We insist that in order to render intelligent analysis of anything, the subject must be studied if the analysis is to have value. We further submit that the only qualifications necessary to criticize, are a few discordant thoughts and the ability to speak or write. We do not agree that parrot-like repetition of prejudices equals intelligent analysis.

Then comes the reference in the article to a "fourth level device" devised by a Western Astrologer in which it is asserted that he advanced the theory that men and women whose birthdays are two months apart shouldn't be married. This is very interesting because it was not a Western Astrologer who dug through divorce records, but a Western Attorney, John A. Hadaller (who, to the best of our knowledge, is still an attorney and not an astrologer).

Contrary to the false assertion relative to the two months, the sixty day period on his graph does not show it to be unfavorable but favorable for marriage. We have an article by Mr. Hadaller before us as we write in which he states: "During thirteen years of research attempting to find the cause or factor of divorce, I have discovered a remarkable parallelism between basic facts and the ancient tenents of astrology." The article was published in National Astrological Journal for February 1934. Thus this is not a new gimmick as is claimed and the facts are entirely different than represented. This appears as a distortion of the record.

We are not aware that statistical research has become unscientific, and we contradict the intimation that investigation of a subject (any subject including astrology) by statistical or other methods is dangerous. We do not believe in thought control. We do not advocate that anyone blindly accept anything we say or teach. On the contrary, we encourage independent thinking.

A number of years ago we kept three books at hand, books written by three well-known scientists. We used these books to point out to students the danger of blind acceptance without analysis, because we view this attitude of blind acceptance as the greatest bar to human progress.

Leaping to conclusions does not indicate the ability to think. On the contrary, it is our contention that people who think, consider to the best of their ability all of the factors which enter into the particular subject under consideration, carefully analyze the evidence available and draw conclusions after analysis.

Your investigator has not torn the veil from astrology. There has never been any veil over it. We submit, however, that he has unveiled one of the most remarkable sets of unwarranted assumptions and conclusions that has ever come to our attention. We also submit that whenever any honest investigation of anything takes place that all of the facts—favorable as well as unfavorable—must be considered.

When emotions, harmonious or discordant, are much in evidence, the ability to analyze and arrive at correct conclusions is not and cannot be in evidence at one and the same time. In order to determine facts, analysis must be dispassionate.

We think that we are rendering a public service in presenting our teachings. We endeavor to be as factual as is possible. We do not think we need to apologize for any part of them. Nor do we think it necessary to turn the other cheek when a so obviously biased and unfair attack such as this occurs.

Cordially,
EDWARD DOANE
President

Intelligence can only be present when the mind possessing it is capable of completely dispassionate analysis of any subject under consideration. What is written in any book, or set of books, including the Brotherhood of Light Lessons, is Information. Information can become Knowledge only when (if correct information) the individual proves it to be true to himself.

Blind acceptance of anything, without critical analysis, is a sure way to know nothing of the subject. Thus being able to repeat what some so-called authority has written or said, indicates no intelligence whatsoever. Any recording instrument is able to repeat most faithfully.

Had authority been correct in the past, we would have no photography, no electric lights, no commercial air lines and a multitude of other things.

We possess a copy of an article, written in the early days of aviation proving, because of "well-known laws of aerodynamics" that the airplane could never be more than a rich man's toy, and that it could never be used in war because dynamite could not be applied that way.

According to these same well-known laws of aerodynamics, the bumble bee could not fly either. It is fortunate for the bumble bee that he did not have the same scientific education as the noted authority.

When anyone blindly accepts a prejudice against anything that is a legitimate object or field of investigation, including astrology, religion, the human mind, or almost anything else, that person is insuring his or her own ignorance and implanting a psychological block in his mind which distorts everything pertaining to the subject that enters the mind. This block acts as a subconscious censor, for one has served notice to himself, by suggestion, that facts are not wanted. Thus the blind acceptance of prejudice is an effective bar to intellectual and spiritual progress.

When some university professor, who has blindly accepted a prejudice against astrology, attempts to pass on that prejudice to his students, he is ignorant, and working against the welfare (intellectual and spiritual) of the class members.

And, as is true in the case of one professor who appealed for help in "killing it off," whether the professor knows it or not, he is advocating burning the records and slaughtering all who have knowledge of the subject (since astrology resides in the minds of men and women). We do not think he knows what he is advocating, because all we have read of his effort does not indicate that he knows anything about the functional usage of words.

Words mean something only when translated into functional terms. To accomplish work of any kind, energy must be expended. Energy can be expended only in contact (connection) with some existing form of substance. The combined action and reaction produce change in form.

The fact that the above mentioned individual who wants to kill it (astrology) off does not to this day have the slightest idea of just what he wants to kill off, well shows the damage that can be done to a mind through the blind acceptance of prejudice.

A psychologist recently witnessed some genuine psychic phenomena. When asked what he thought about it, he replied, "I would believe anything else on one-tenth the evidence, but I would not believe that on ten times the evidence." This attitude shows the uselessness of offering evidence to a person so prejudiced that facts relevant to the subject cannot enter the mind without distortion. In other words, it is useless to "cast pearls before swine."

Crafty men, such as Hitler and Stalin, have fostered prejudice and ignorance. By using the same propaganda techniques that have been used in attacking astrology, they succeeded in bringing misery to millions of people. Whether it is a professor in a university, a rabble rouser of the extreme right or left, some religious leader, or an editor who employs these techniques he is attempting to keep the populace in ignorance and foster prejudice. He is working against human progress and enlightenment.

Any mind that deliberately distorts facts is not an intelligent mind, no matter how many university degrees the person possessing the mind may have. The intelligent mind earnestly searches for truth—regardless of what truth may be. It seeks to eliminate prejudice and gain understanding of its problems, to gain knowledge of what it must do to make progress, and to determine its relationship to other persons and to God. The proof of intelligence is always true intellectual integrity.

An intelligent person does not want to deceive self or anyone else. The crafty person, on the contrary, fosters ignorance and prejudice, for only thus can he control and gain power over his fellows. If the people in question gain true intelligence, they will see that what was called authority proved, more often than not, to be in error.

The only way that civilization can make progress is through the displacement of ignorance with knowledge and the displacement of prejudice with enlightened understanding. It is the function of The Church of Light to provide as much accurate information as possible so that more and more people can gain understanding and eliminate prejudice.

Civilization advances in direct proportion to the ability of people to think for themselves, to determine truth for themselves, and to fulfill their Divine destiny. This can be accomplished only through factual education and the acceptance of individual responsibility.

The amount of aid we can give in helping build a new and better civilization depends to a large degree upon the amount of people we can reach with The Brotherhood of Light Teachings. All people should strive to make the world in which we live a better place through the abolition of poverty and through developing and spreading information about the spiritual pathway.

We are going to do all we can, at any given time, to dispel the shrouding darkness of ignorance and prejudice that made the previous dark ages possible. In this effort, we need all of the help we can get. We work to help build a new and better civilization. It is thus that we can aid present and future generations of mankind, and it is thus that we can be of value to God through assisting the Divine Plan of Progressive Evolution toward Eternal Light.

HOW ASTROLOGY WORKS

AN ASTROLOGICAL Chart is a map of the chief vibratory factors in nature as they exist at a given place at a given moment in time.

The association of the chart with a child born at the same place and time is a purely arbitrary association, just as any and all mathematical association is arbitrary. It is a valid association only because the basic urges (planets) and more loosely organized thought cells (signs) of the subconscious mental organism (soul) of the child equal in basic key tone the planetary and sign vibration equivalent.

Mundane houses of the chart map the departments of life with which these urges and other elements are associated. The zodiacal signs equal motivating factors which may be called principles. The decanate divisions of the signs map specialized trends given to these motivating factors. The planets (including Sun and Moon for convenience in handling) map the basic urges or thought families. Aspects between the planets equal thought compounds. An association between two or more of the basic urges (planets) in a painful or pleasurable manner is mapped by the so-called good or bad aspects.

Since Nature is always in tune, in harmony, and discord, at any given place and time, the above is valid.

Progression (directions)—major, minor and transit—map periods of time when the subconscious mind is tuned in on energies of the planets involved in the aspect or aspects mapped. Progressions map times when more than usual energy is being received from planetary sources.

What happens under the aspect or aspects depends upon three things: (1) the basic character as mapped by the chart; (2) the conditioning energy built into the subconscious mind by response to stimuli since birth, and

(3) the environment in which the person functions and its resistance to happenings of a given type or types.

The value of astrology lies in the fact that one is able to predict the time, type and relative volume of energy that will be received from planetary sources for any number of years ahead. With this information, he can take precautionary actions to avoid unnecessary discord and possible tragedy. He can plan ahead of the aspect and decide how to use the energy constructively in achieving physical, intellectual and spiritual progress.

Thus far Natal Astrology might safely be called scientific, both in concept and practice. However, when one attempts to estimate the result in terms of specific event, or when one deals with other than mental and emotional stimuli, we think such practice is an art.

According to our estimates, the energy received from planetary sources by the unconscious mind of an individual is about one-fourth of the total energy of the mind. Another fourth comes from character radiations (one-eighth), including talismanic gems, and to the thoughts of others (one-eighth). The remaining one-half comes from his own thoughts and feelings.

If a person has developed a vigorous will and has learned to use directed thinking and induced emotion, the energies of the mind (including those received from planetary sources) can be brought under control and directed into channels of his own choosing. He can, to a large degree, determine what will happen under a given set of aspects. This is genuine Free Will.

When the Natal Chart is used in this manner, it provides an excellent road map that helps to determine when and how to use the powers of the mind to be more successful than is possible when one travels without direction.

We believe that the life goal of everyone should be to learn how to be an ever more constructive unit in the service of God, working to assist the fulfillment of the Divine Plan of Eternal Progression.

Using Natal Astrology as an aid to understanding self and the proper relationship of self to others and to God is a most constructive use of the road map. By so doing a person can obtain genuine free will and become master of his fate and captain of his soul. This is the pathway to true freedom.

In following the pathway to freedom, we view the study of Esoteric Psychology and Mental Alchemy as essentials in understanding the subconscious mental organism and thus Natal Astrology.

As we stated above, the association of the chart with a child born at the place and time for which the chart is erected is a purely arbitrary association. No one can tell from looking at the chart whether or not it was erected for a horary question, the start of some venture, the birth of a dog or a human, or whether it was a time chosen haphazardly for an example chart with no particular association.

Our useage of the basic keytone relationship is valid, because all sensory perception is an interpretation of frequencies by the mental organism. As these urges are groups of frequencies, they—like the frequency radiations of the planets—obviously have a basic key tone. This theory (if you wish) we regard as proven and provable by any one wishing to do the work involved. We regard this procedure as scientifically sound as that used in any other science.

The above is a brief resume of our view of one facet of astrology. The person who desires to study and use this type of Natal Astrology for the purposes of becoming a happier, more useful, and more successful member of earth and cosmic society should study The Brotherhood of Light Lessons.

In all of our research, we use the common or Placidian tables of houses. Daltons, American Astrology, Rosicrucian Fellowship, Aries Press and Raphaels are all of this type.

We have been asked about other tables and about the so-called equal area system of house division. We do not use these systems for what seems to us to be valid reasons.

The acid test of a Natal Chart and its correctness does not lie in argument about this or that system of house division, but in whether or not the basic urges—mapped by planetary factors in the chart—function in relationship to the department of life (house) in which they are placed in the chart. And in whether or not they function in relationship to the department of life mapped by progressions—major, minor and transit.

Thus far in our experience with research embracing many thousands of timed charts (we do not use rectified or speculative charts in research), we have found the Placidian system of house division to be accurate. Therefore we do not believe it would be constructive to throw away all of the research we have done, and are doing, merely because someone advances differing theories.

All theories must remain unsubstantiated until extensive research proves them valid. Our view is that the theories we hold have been proven and are capable of being proven by any one willing to do the work involved.

We have been asked about the fixed zodiac and have seen a few charts indicating that evidence adduced from transits appeared to validate the claim. However, progressions were not used in these few cases, and since in the Hermetic System of Astrology we do use progressions with the charts of nations and cities as well as individuals, our opinion is that the evidence is so superficial that it proves or disproves nothing.

In the Hermetic System of Astrology everything used in the chart has its equivalent in the subconscious mental organism of the human being. We are convinced that this correspondence between the chart and the human is an absolute necessity if we desire to call our system scientific, and we do.

We do not use the Moon's Nodes, fixed stars, the part of fortune (and other parts and nodes), midpoints or other supposed factors in the chart because we have been unable to find any correspondence whatsoever between these elements and the subconscious mental organism of the human being. Nor have we been able to find anywhere that the advocates of these elements have established such essential correspondence.

A symbol is that which stands for something. Something, in turn, can only be defined as some form of energy, matter or motion in some time-space relationship. Therefore, we are convinced that the figures and symbols used in a Natal Chart must equal something in the subconscious mental organism of the person for whom the chart is erected, or they stand for nothing at all and therefore are invalid in theory and useage in any system deserving to be called scientific.

We wish to make clear at this point that we believe in the freedom of others to hold and advance any theories they desire. If we believed otherwise, we could not believe in freedom for all, as we do.

Some have said, "Progressions do not work." One person who made such a statement used a system that did not progress the slower moving planets, thus missing a Jupiter conjunction Sun and opposed by progressed Saturn. He had progressed Jupiter but not Saturn. Consequently, when the expected Santa Claus turned out to be a period of loss, he said progressions did not work and never used them again. He never realized that he had not used them at all except in a half-measure sort of way. Because his system neglected important elements, it was invalid.

A progression does work by adding energy to the subconscious mind. If one does not understand what "working" means and deals with a superficial or shallow type of astrology, his statements hardly have sufficient validity to warrant serious consideration. And furthermore, unless opinions are backed by considerable research, they are just opinions and nothing more.

A vast amount of work has been done to date in the never ending task of astrological research, which will ultimately yield much valuable information. Some of our present ideas may be modified by new information thus gained. But of one factor we are certain, our basic working hypothesis will not be changed. That is the correctness of the Basic Key Tone Relationship between planetary factors and the subconscious mind which allows for the transmission of energy under the Law of Resonance, which is sometimes called the Law of Sympathetic Vibratory Response.

We view this astrological research as a very essential part of our program and one that holds much promise for making Astrology practical and useful to future generations. It is our desire to learn as much as we can of this Golden Key so that humanity may obtain the maximum possible benefit from its useage.

We are convinced that each soul is an independent entity, working out its own salvation and that its mission on earth is to gain love and wisdom, so that self conscious immortality may be obtained. And that realizing self conscious immortality, become of its own free will and accord a constructive unit in the Divine Plan of Eternal Progression. We are convinced that the study and constructive application of the Hermetic System of Natal Astrology as we teach it can be a powerful aid in this exalted aim as well as invaluable assistance in understanding and solving the more earthy problems of everyday life.

In the last analysis, each soul must learn to rely upon itself for the apprehension of truth. To accept blindly without analysis or discrimination the statements of others, including ourselves, as truth is to adopt the attitude of uncritical mysticism. And it is this habit of uncritical mysticism—the blind acceptance of so-called authority as the arbiter of truth—that is the greatest bar to human progress—individual, racial and national.

Initiative and decisive, positive actions are necessary to every soul. With positive thinking and acting come the willingness to accept responsibility for one's own errors of thinking and consequent action.

Too often the students of shallow versions of astrology will build a habit-system of saying, "I cannot do this, that or the other, because Saturn or some other planet, is so and so in my chart." They attempt to place the responsibility for their own inadequacies upon the radiations of a body far distant in the sky. It is exactly equal to saying, "I am a slave! I do not control my thinking, and I do not want to do so."

Students of astrology as well as other people including those in orthodox religious groups too often look for some convenient scapegoat to blame for their own lack of adult intelligence and emotional reaction and try to avoid at all costs the work of learning to think, feel and act for self and accept the responsibility for such thinking, feeling and acting.

Until they make drastic changes in their habits of thinking, feeling and acting, these poor people have blindly accepted slavery to authority as the preferred method of life, never realizing that no soul can be free until it is determined to think, feel and act for self, and to accept full responsibility for its own errors. It is the pathway to spiritual greatness and the epitome of human achievement.

All energies are good energies, regardless of source or of how they are mapped in an astrological chart. It is the control and direction given these energies by the mind and the emotional reaction that accompanies their reception and useage which determines whether constructive or destructive work is accomplished by them. For this reason, it is not so much what we have in our charts as what we do with what we have that determines the effect upon ourselves and, to a very large degree, the physical events that come into our lives.

All relationships in life ultimately resolve down to energy receptions, transmissions and consequent changes produced in form. Any relationship with anything becomes in some manner an energy relationship. Viewing a beautiful sunset is the reception and interpretation of frequency rates—a form of energy reception. Loving some one and being loved in return is an energy exchange involving radiation and reception of energy.

Even the relationship to God resolves down to an energy relationship involving radiation and reception of energies from this exalted source. And relationships to any power, including God, entail relationships with all manifestations of that power, including the part of Creation we call the solar system, and hence the reason that astrology might be properly called, when correctly conceived and used, a divine science.

But to assume that all that is called astrology is so used or deserves to be called scientific in operation is to accept error for fact. For one may use astrology for fortune telling. Positive prediction of events is impossible because of free will.

Because of the large amount of classified material available, astrology, in general, is a science. Some applications follow scientific procedure and thus are scientific. Others do not follow scientific procedure and are thus artistic instead of scientific. Consequently, the practice of astrology may be either an art of a science, depending upon the basic assumption and type of procedure.

No one has a monopoly on truth. Truth is universal property. Each soul is continually evolving and ultimately gaining in intelligence, and in love and wisdom. Absolute truth is always just ahead—a goal toward which we eternally travel but never reach. For as our understanding expands, so does our mind grasp more facets of the absolute. We realize that this expansion and gaining in understanding and in usefulness to the Creator is an eternal process, and that the Absolute that is God is always ahead. While we reach that God in consciousness and receive divine inspiration, the total understanding is always and eternally ahead in the Divine Plan.

Advancing more and more, we realize that God acts only through the expenditures of energy in producing eternal change in existing forms of substance and influencing the minds of man along such channels as will yield response to divine desire, thus producing changes in civilization that, in the long run, add up to progress and to the fulfillment of the Divine Plan of Eternal Progression.

It is quite common for people of little or no understanding of God and his plan to say that God could not do this, that or the other. Such people make totally false assumptions as to what God wants. They have never made a study of what God does. Nor do they realize that there is only one ultimate Source of Power, one Source of Law, One Divine Plan and One Absolute in whom and of whom we are.

Like God, man should learn to think and act unceasingly, doing all that is possible with the equipment he has to do with at any given time, to further the cause of human enlightenment as to the physical, intellectual and spiritual nature of human kind and the true relation of human kind to the Creator.

The potential of the human soul is unlimited. The development of that potential requires effort: that is, the expenditure of energy in expanding the consciousness, gaining understanding, love and wisdom, and realizing and taking up the individual cosmic work. This requires gaining self control, self reliance, the acceptance of one's own responsibilities and learning to be of use to God.

Seek and ye shall find. Knock and it shall be opened unto you. Lack of understanding is the curtain that hides the beautiful reality of one's spiritual origin and destiny from the individual consciousness. Therefore, with all thy getting, get understanding.

As an aid to gaining self understanding, learning to understand others, and of knowing the true relationship of man to God, the Hermetic System of Natal Astrology is of inestimable value.

ENERGY CAPTURE, STORAGE, RELEASE

THE ROOSTER is convinced that he is a very important fellow. He sits on the fence or other prominent object early every morning and tries to tell the world just how big and important he really is.

Of course, the rooster isn't aware that he is expressing his drive for significance. Obviously he hasn't analyzed the situation to find out the types of energies he expresses or the source of these energies. Still he is convinced he is very important and that he is a great authority on the matter.

You and I are a bit higher up the scale. We have studied some, thought some, and perhaps even engaged in a degree of analytical thinking. For instance, we might have determined—in one way or another—that the magical tetragramatton of the ancients, the Jod He Vau He, is the basis of all truly analytical thinking. When this Jod He Vau He is expressed as the One Principle (Energy), the One Law (Polarity, or Action and Reaction), the One Agent (Form) and the One Truth (Reality), it gives us the basic key necessary to make our Mercury (mind) a true Hermes, or messenger of the God within.

Assuming that we all have so determined this, perhaps you won't mind listening a while so that I can talk to you quite informally, just as though we were sitting in comfortable chairs together, indulging in a friendly chat. In this manner we can feel easy and relaxed.

As a human being, you have a Body (form) and a Mind, as well as an Ego, or Spirit. Like other humans your mind—conscious and subconscious—is your soul.

Your Spirit (Ego) is the energizing spark of Deity that constitutes the God within. The Ego is the creative energy that brought the soul, you, into being. It is the prime source of the power that causes you and other souls to struggle along—even when like the rooster you do not know why or what for.

Whatever affects the biological or psychological You does so through an expenditure of energy. This energy, like all other energies, must have a source. It must obey the laws governing the transmission of the particular type of energy involved.

If you have studied "Esoteric Psychology" and "Mental Alchemy" (as well as a few more Brotherhood of Light Courses), you are aware of the basic urges of the subconscious mind, and of the keytone relationships. You are also aware of the similar keytone relationships of the astral radiations of the planets and the zodiacal signs. This relationship allows the Law of Resonance to operate, making it possible for you to receive—albeit subconsciously—astrological energies which stimulate given types of thought, feeling and action.

In turn—since your motion under stimulus in the environment in which you function causes reaction from that environment—the types of thought, feeling and action determine to a large degree the physical, mental and emotional events of your life.

Because you possess the potential of changing your habit-systems of thinking, feeling and acting—and, therefore, changing the action and reaction of environment—you have the power to change destiny in the physical as well as in the soul sense.

But the main point here is just this: Whatever effects your thinking, feeling and acting, consequently your life, must of necessity be the result of some sort of energy being captured, stored and released by you. Since energies must travel under law, there must be some resonant point in your subconscious mind (or soul) that responds to such energies. If there is no resonant point, obviously the energies are not received and do not affect you.

Let's catch our breaths for a moment and realize that after all, we are trying to find out what makes us tick like we do. We are trying to find the means of avoiding error in our thinking. I am assuming that as a thinking, feeling human being, you are interested in avoiding such errors as would hinder the progress of your soul and prohibit your realization of your Divine Origin, Mission and Destiny.

Perhaps I had better digress a moment to state an occult truth: So long as you depend upon something or someone outside of yourself to be the supreme authority in anything, that long will you fail to make progress and fail to develop and realize the vast potentials resident in your Divine Self. Authority equals stagnation.

I have previously illustrated how authorities cannot always be depended upon. I used to keep three books on my desk to show students the danger of allowing anyone else to do their thinking for them.

One book was "The Evolution of Physics," by Einstein and Infield, wherein a serious error occurred regarding the energies necessary to wave propagation. The second was "The Nature of The Physical World," by Sir Arthur Eddington, whose attempt to explain why a table held up a piece of paper failed. The other was "Electrons, Plus and Minus," by Robert A. Millikan, who apparently disproved Erhenhaft's conclusions as to the existence of a sub-electron. But in explaining the effect of the B-ray on the atoms through which it passed, he stated, "It simply shakes loose some electronic dust." Electronic dust means sub-electron if it means anything.

A recent press item quoted scientist Fritz Swicky as having a scheme of colonizing Jupiter with earth people.

The main job in the project concerned changing the orbit of Jupiter to make the climate more pleasant for human habitation. According to the press story, this was to be brought about by shooting Jupiter with a huge H bomb and blasting it into a new orbit. This theory overlooked an obvious fact. The earth has already been blasted by several H bombs and its orbit hasn't changed.

I use these examples to show how authority can be in error. The main purpose of this talk with you is to try to convince you of the tremendous importance of learning to do your own thinking, and learning to be your own sole authority on the validity of any statements, whether in science or religion.

All people—whether kings or commoners, scientists or religious potentates, even as you and I—have a similar physiological, psychological and spiritual make up. All are subject to possible error, no matter how great the world may think they are. None are so important that the world cannot get along without them, because in time it must so get along. Therefore, you and I are not unique, we have a lot of company.

Just now in the astrological world, much ado is being made about this and that. One person writes, in effect, that it is not necessary to consider specific energies, etc.—that astrology can be an abstract mathematical expression. Now just what does that mean? To me, it means completely divorcing astrology from reality—from any practical value, thus making it useless and confusing.

Remember the Jod He Vau He: the One Principle, the One Law, the One Agent, the One Truth. Nothing happens, nothing exists, without the capture, storage and release of energy. All that is, was, or ever will be is expressed in that basic formula. As everything functions as energy, matter and motion in some time-space relationship, this precludes abstract mathematical expression.

Another writer introduces 66 new astrological points. Not one of them is related to anything within the mental or physical organism of the human being, for whom a chart is supposed to be erected and interpreted. Not one of them is related to energy, therefore none has any specific meaning in the life of the individual. Is this scientific? Or is it merely another form of abstract mathematical expression? To me, it is meaningless, except perhaps in some form of fortune telling, where many symbols are needed to stimulate the subconscious organism of the reader.

One of the prolific astrological writers stated in print, "We cannot have a dynamics of astrology." In the same article, he said that astrology was all symbolic. So I wrote to him, pointing out the fact that a symbol is that which stands for something. Something, in turn, can only be defined as some phase of energy, matter or motion in a time-space relationship. Therefore, we either had a dynamics of astrology or we had nothing at all.

"I am willing to admit privately," he replied, "that there is a dynamics of astrology." To this day, he has not admitted this belief in public. Is this integrity? Yet many people think he is just wonderful as he goes on inventing new types of charts that are completely without meaning.

Then there are others who are also like roosters who want to tell the world what great and wonderful fellows they are. They sit on the astrological fence and do a lot of crowing. They hasten to advise us that all astrology has been seriously in error up to their own marvelous advent upon this earth. They tell us that the wonderful work they are doing is sure to correct all of us and show us how foolish we actually are.

None of these disciples of confusion are being very friendly to genuine astrology. Yet I am sure they will all insist that they desire to get astrology accepted by the so-called scientists and take its rightful place as a valuable adjunct to human understanding.

Still they persist in failing to recognize that a correct basis of mathematical equivalents and energy relationships must be established if astrology is to be genuinely useful to a human being and to ultimately take its place as a genuine science.

A case in point is the fixed zodiac. If I understand the theory correctly, it will be necessary for millions upon millions of people to change the basic makeup of their subconscious minds in order to make this theory valid. Wouldn't it be interesting to observe a lot of Virgo people struggling in vain to become Leo people? In my belief, this is an insurmountable difficulty. I am quite sure that such psychological change will not take place, no matter how much the devotees of the various fixed zodiacs insist **upon it.**

Crowing roosters, crowing scientists, crowing people, crowing astrologers all have one thing in common—a hereditary drive for significance. It reminds me of what Elbert Benjamine said when he received a letter from a lady telling of how many important positions she had held at one time or another: "The lady boasts, therefore, she is ignorant."

Then there are the enemies of astrology—unable to repeal the Law of Resonance—who have tried but failed to convince the public that there is nothing to astrology. They've been trying to do it for thousands of years. The public, having sufficient intellectual rebels among its members, has always insisted upon believing that which it could test and find true. Good examples are found in the history of photography, or the prediction that "someday electricity will light a house."

Creative thinkers through the centuries have dared to question the validity of so-called authority. They are responsible for every advance that has been made in human learning. And we who are determined to become free souls must also question authority—must test and prove or disprove things for ourselves. This approach is necessary if we ever hope to find and follow our own individual missions in life—to find the God Within.

Know Yourself, Be Yourself, and Give Yourself. This is an admonition which, if practiced, can lead you to a much greater happiness, usefulness and spirituality than you ever dreamed possible. But, the only type of astrology that can assist you to know yourself and be yourself with an ever increasing scope of intelligence and happiness, is an astrology which has established equivalents in your subconscious or soul self.

Neither your biological nor your psychological selves are abstract mathematical expressions. Every moment of being represents some type of thought, feeling and action in this business of living. The energies and mechanics of this thought, feeling and action can be understood and utilized by you providing only: (1) That you are willing to do your own thinking. (2) That you direct your own feeling and acting, accepting your place in the Divine Plan as a free soul. (3) That you be your own authority, by using, testing and proving the various principles in the laboratory of your own life.

As you must be aware, I am trying to sell you an idea. But the idea does not embrace the blind acceptance of anything. However, it does embrace study, analysis and testing. It does embrace making progress. It does embrace being the potentially Divine You.

The Hermetic System of Astrology is a practical down-to-earth method. It will remain so as long as it provides, in the natal chart, an accurate representation of the chief basic elements of the subconscious mental organism as it existed at birth. And so long as the method of progressions—majors, minors and transits—continue to map the stimuli received from astrological sources will this system remain practical.

Change, when brought about as the result of an advance in understanding, can be highly constructive. That is why we engage as vigorously as we can in continued astrological research. And we expect to do a great deal more research throughout the years. As a matter of fact, we expect what we are doing along these lines to continue through the coming centuries and yield much valuable new information.

Of course, being human beings on the pathway of Eternal life, we are not perfect. Perfection is an ever advancing goal which we never reach but toward which we continually strive. As our understanding advances or intellectual horizons widen, new facets are constantly coming into the view finder of our ideal of perfection.

Astrology, as we now understand it, is the Golden Key to gaining knowledge of self. To put the thought into terms which conceal from the profane but reveal to the true aspirant to occult initiation: it is the keystone to the Ninth Arch, the Living Arch in the structure of the Temple of the Soul.

Those dealing with human bodies and human minds, whether from the standpoint of science or religion, who reject this keystone and try to hide it under the rubbish of ignorance and the trash of bigotry and prejudice, without realizing it, are trying to block the progress of humanity toward Eternal Light.

You and I have not rejected the keystone, and we invite others, with a desire to obey the ancient admonition "Know Yourself," to use this key to self understanding. Along with the Golden Key (astrology), we use the Silver Key (the tarot) and all of the associated wisdom that goes with the two keys to find the solution to life's problems and to help find the God Within.

True importance is gained through spiritual progression and contributing something of value to the Divine Plan. Pride in such an accomplishment is justified and is constructive satisfaction for the drive for significance. Boasting or crowing is for the ignorant and for roosters.

ASTROLOGY AND HEALTH

PHYSICAL life has but one purpose. That is to enable each individual soul to gather such a harvest of experiences as will enable one to gain ultimate love and wisdom to the end that self-conscious immortality may be attained, and enable one to enter into a comprehensive cooperation with other forces of light in the furtherance of God's Great Plan of Eternal Progression.

Now you may ask, "What has this to do with astrology and health?" Certainly the question is a fair one.

To the extent the available energies, at any given time, are directed to the accomplishment of some work that adds to the richness or length of life in the physical sense, and to the richness of life as a whole, the soul is functioning in accordance with the Cosmic Moral Code.

The arrangement and strength of the thought families, mapped by the planets in the natal chart, gives one a comprehensive picture of the tools that a person has to work with in this phase of existence. The discordant aspects in the chart represent the distinctive lessons each needs to learn, as well as pointing out the method that will work best in transmuting the mapped discord into harmony. The attainment and maintenance of physical health is a distinctive aid; but it is not enough. For one may have physical health and function as a happy-go-lucky sort of person, who fails utterly to make appreciable progression while here.

Mental alchemy offers the method of reconditioning the thought families so that one will be more fortunate and more healthy. Yet it is entirely possible for one to practice mental alchemy for better health and better fortune without making any particular spiritual progression. It is the spiritual health, or lack of it, that is the most important to the soul as an individualized function, and to the race as a whole, both the visible and invisible parts of it.

Anyone who can erect and progress his own chart finds it relatively easy to note each aspect—major, minor, and transit, and check his own reactions to the stimuli received. By noting the best and worst manifestations of each sign and planet as given in Zain's Natal Astrology, the determination of whether the reaction is constructive or destructive is not hard. All that is required is a sincere desire to know the truth relative to one's self.

In this manner, with the practice of mental alchemy, the discords can be gradually eliminated, so far as physical reactions are concerned. But if one perceives the Eternal Now is all that he will ever have to work with, and the desire is to make as much soul progression as possible, then a different outlook is necessary, and the aspect and the reactions will be considered from the angle of soul progression. Embracing a still wider field than spiritual alchemy, is Cosmic Alchemy, in which the reactions to the stimuli are considered solely as to how much of a contribution is made to universal welfare.

In short, the chart of birth and progressed chart offer a certain mathematical means of checking spiritual progress. No one need remain in the dark as to whether or not he actually is making progress in the spiritual sense, or as to whether or not he has sharpened and improved the tools he was given at birth.

To me, this angle of Astrology is of prime importance and needs consideration along with the rest when we think of health. Total health is much more than a physical manifestation.

Because of our evolutionary inheritances, we like to rationalize and twist conditions around, so that we can satisfy our hereditary drive for significance; for we like to Be Something in the eyes of our fellows. Many times, people connected with some occult organization imagine they are being spiritual; when the truth is they are sailing along under sextiles and trines, only to be somewhat leveled when a square or opposition comes along. Then the plaint is, "Why did this have to happen to me, when I have tried to live right?"

All of which means that when the time for testing comes along, the opportunity for real spiritual progress is lost because of the destructive mental attitude. Were it not for the obstacles and so-called bad aspects in the chart, we would in all probability retrograde spiritually instead of progressing.

Gaining the Cosmic Viewpoint is not done without the expenditure of energy. The energies available must be directed toward the accomplishment of this desirable end. Neither is it done in a day. For it is a long step from the common viewpoint of looking at all things as important only as affecting self, to that of looking at all things and self as important only as affecting life as a whole. Yet that method is the cosmic method, and the one which will allow the individual to ultimately attain complete mastery of mind and emotions, and realize his purpose in life, here and hereafter.

Once the cosmic viewpoint is attained, and effort made to maintain it, noticeable growth takes place. Individual problems shrink into insignificance by relative comparison.

If we are to become practitioners of cosmic alchemy, rendering a contribution to universal welfare and the Health of the Cosmos in the largest sense, then it is necessary for us to forget personalities as being of prime importance, and to view the welfare and progress of the whole as the matter of greatest moment in our lives.

As soon as the individual adopts the habit of thinking in terms of cosmic welfare and starts to view his or her life as important only as affecting that welfare, personal troubles shrink to the vanishing point.

Considered from the purely individual viewpoint, which is the saturnine angle, little things, incapable of creating a ripple on the stream of life as a whole, assume a magnitude that eclipses the problems of the whole. The sense of proportion is much distorted, and the glorious Sun of True Spirituality is hidden from us. Only because we are hiding our heads under the bushel of self consideration. Adopting the Cosmic Viewpoint as a regular habit of mind shows up minor shadows for what they are; and the Sun of Eternal Light is continuously within the bounds of vision.

All factors of life are conditioned by pleasure or pain. Hence in making a change from one habit system of thinking, feeling and action, it is necessary to associate pleasure with the new habit system.

In the cosmic sense, this can best be done by realizing what pleasure is. If the actions provide a guide for reality, pleasure is experienced. Most people mistake the pleasures of the moment for real pleasure. Usually what is called pleasure in the physical sense turns out to have an ultimate painful reaction, proving that the individual did not know what real pleasure was.

The real joys of life are those which persist throughout eternity. They can only be attained by rendering constructive, wholly unselfish service in the interest of universal welfare.

We have a great amount of mental and spiritual disease in the world, manifesting destructively as warfare, riots, intolerance, etc. This is caused by racial and national destructive reaction to the stimuli received in the world chart. Of course it is unnecessary, since it is just as easy to spend energies constructively. It is the method in which these energies are expended that determines the reaction—individual, national or racial. One way lies progress; the other, retrogression.

In the interest of mental and spiritual health then, it is the part of wisdom to view each aspect from the Physical, Mental and Spiritual angle. All are interrelated in the problems of life. And in building a physical body through corrective feeding, to help ourselves to become enabled to capture, store and release more energy, and therefore accomplish more work in the interest of universal welfare.

The study of astrology is unending, and the amount of information a chart can be made to reveal, literally astounding. For, as Fred H. Skinner, co-founder of The Church of Light, once wrote me, "We no sooner gain one interpretation, until a new one unfolds before us." That is entirely true.

Soul Color Scheme

"How can I determine the degree of my own constructive thinking?" A fair question. One that is sure to arise in every sincere student's mind.

Harmonious function of the glandular system, and the consequent efficient handling by the system of the various chemical elements and vitamins, depends on the state of the thought families in the mind that correspond to the glands and the planets. In Zain's "Natal Astrology" is given the best and worst qualities associated with each thought family (mapped by a planet).

We might ally these thought families to their corresponding colors and then use black and white as the extremes of constructive positive manifestation (white) and the extremes of destructive negative manifestation (black), and assert the problem in terms of clarity of tone of color with due attention to the octave relationship of Uranus, Neptune and Pluto in this method of illustration.

By this method we can visualize what we are actually doing with ourselves in terms of Physical, Mental and Spiritual Health as we watch the stimulation and interpret our reactions from our natal and progressed planetary positions. With each thought, feeling and action we are dipping our brush into the colors of life that correspond to the physical colors of the spectrum, and the positive white and the negative black that constitute the polarities of color.

Obviously, the more of the black or negative thought, feeling and action we use in our painting, the more muddy tones we are putting in the canvas of the soul and the more adverse reaction we are getting in terms of physical health.

Take the Sun, Orange, Power Urge, Stimuli. If we gain the ability to Rule and exert such Rulership as is justified with full realization of the effect in terms of universal welfare, our Orange Tones possess all of the beauty and texture of the refined gold of the spiritual alchemist. Because the Power Urges are at their best and strongest under this type of rulership, a subsequent healthy reaction can be expected in the anterior (front) pituitary so far as its thyroid relationship is concerned and upon the thyroid in its pituitary and heart relationship.

If on the other hand we assume the Dictative attitude and are determined to rule or ruin and have no consideration for the welfare of others or what they may think about the matter and do not care what happens just so long as we can be Boss; then we are mixing the Black with our Orange and taking an attitude that may for a time, if we mix sufficient Red (Mars, Aggressive Urges) with it, prove a powerful stimulus to the corresponding glands as given above, produce an inevitable effect through wearing out by overwork discordant thought in terms of breakdown of these functions and pay the bill in physical terms as well as soul terms. For what we put on our canvas does not make for a beautiful clear-toned picture of the soul. From the spiritual angle, instead of clearing our Gold of Dross we are adding more Dross to it and rendering the metal impure. Somewhat the reverse of any refining process.

The Green of our soul color scheme and physical body color scheme is the Moon, or in terms of thought families, the Domestic Urge. The positive or White side of this manifestation is adaptability; or the ability to make the best of such circumstances as we may find ourselves in to work for a happy family relationship, using whatever materials are at hand. But do not mistake me here, for this can well be done with a weather eye out for any possibilities of bettering existing circumstances and at one and the same time do the best we can with what we have to work with. If we do this, our spiritual silver will be well refined and on its way to the final blend and transmutation into spiritual gold. Our colors on the canvas of the soul will blend into the picture as God's Nature Green at its best. The water-salt balance under the posterior (back) pituitary gland will be easier to keep in order, and the thymus gland and lympathic systems will function as they should. It goes without saying, the stomach will not get upset so easily.

On the other hand, if we take the Inconstancy or Black side of our Domestic Urges, and Green, then we will be like the tides running in and out—failing to fulfill our obligations and duties, not sticking to any one line of endeavor long enough to do anything much with it; being impatient and over-emotional, moody and depressed. As a consequence, in mixing our soul Green we put muddy ugly tones on the canvas we are painting and the corresponding physical upsets become quite common occurrences.

Following the laws of nature, Violet is a part of the color spectrum even as the parathyroid glands and the nervous system are part of the physical body. The Intellectual Urges (Mercury-Violet) express on the White side as Expression and the realization that to attain Expression one must study the subjects whatever they may be so that knowledge of them may be attained. In doing so, the beautiful Violet tones blend into the picture of the soul we are painting in perfect harmony with the whole, and our spiritual Mercury reaches transmutation into spiritual gold. As a result, we achieve the Calm collected mental state that assists in keeping the parathyroids functioning and the entire nervous system in order.

We need to realize that any sound structure must start on a sound foundation and be built stone by stone until the building is complete. But if we continually exhibit Restlessness and do not learn Concentration upon a single task or learn to build our Mentalities through feeding them correct mental food, we will fail to follow correct principles with our Violet (Intellectual Urges).

Then we can expect to be restless, nervous, move about without much direction and so add muddy Violet tones to our soul canvas. The picture we are working on every day and every moment will be a hodge-podge of stripes and streaks without having either clarity of tone or correctness of line in any part of it. Our Metallic (spiritual Mercury) will be a mass of poison instead of being made ready to blend into the final transmutation.

Viewing the other thought families (planets) in this relationship will complete our soul color scheme.

Elimination

Anyone who has served with the armed forces has visual evidence of the great changes that can be brought about in the physical structure through deep breathing and exercise. This is because the additional oxygen obtained makes for better combustion of the fuels taken in the form of food, and because regular exercise assists in toning up the entire system, and improving elimination.

All too few people breathe deeply enough to insure sufficient oxygen in the system. Especially is this true of those of us who sit long hours at a desk. Hence it is good to form a habit system of rhythmic breathing, with complete inhalations and exhalations, so that the oxygen needs of the system are fully supplied.

With negative planets in Gemini in the chart, or Mercury afflicted by negative planets, the need to cultivate such a habit is great. When deliberate deep breathing has received sufficient attention, the astral mind will take over the task and keep it up without conscious attention. Also the habit of getting up occasionally, flexing and tensing the muscles, is a good one. The change of position relieves the strain and the attention is directed to other things for a time, giving the mind a rest as well.

In looking at the chart to determine bodily needs, particular attention should be paid to eliminative functions, with intestinal elimination ranking first in relative importance, kidney elimination second, breathing third, and skin fourth.

It is through these eliminative functions that food wastes and accumulated poisons leave the system. If they are retained from any single source, malfunction of some sort is sure to arise. Saturn is chief inhibitor of functions and applies particularly in colon elimination. Neptune is perhaps second in importance as inhibitor because of the extremely negative states produced.

Due attention should always be paid to body areas such as Scorpio and Libra and planets therein when looking to elimination of the kidneys, and in particular to Mars and Pluto, co-rulers of Scorpio. Venus, ruling the skin, affects this area because of its thyroid-gonad relationship, and consequently the hair.

The Sun rules the Vitality in the chart because of its thyroid-pituitary relationship, controlling thereby the basal metabolism rate (fuel handling ability) and the general balancing of the system through the master gland—the front pituitary, which research has determined secretes hormones that have a balancing function in the attempt to counteract imbalance of other glands of the system.

It is this vitality of the system that determines the rapidity of recovery from disease to a large measure. Aspects of Mars to the Sun, whether of the so-called good or bad type, are good since great energy is added by them. Good aspects of Jupiter are excellent, but under the squares, oppositions, etc., the vitality is adversely affected through the tendency to overindulge in rich foods that take their toll through adding an excess of acid residue to the system. This, in turn, works the eliminative organs and helps break down resistance.

Mars afflicts through overwork by the individual, taking its toll through spending too much energy without taking time to recharge.

Mercury, through its Virgo (intestinal) relationship, and rulership of the nervous system as well as the parathyroid glands, is of great importance because the direction given the subconscious mental activities and the type of conscious mental activities enables destructive or harmonious rallying forces from other progressed aspects to add energy, destructive or healing to the areas affected.

The Moon, aside from its back pituitary-thymus relationship, chiefly affects the health through the emotional states engendered, Emotions, combined with thoughts, are the elements that can well be called Basic Causes of Health or Disease, since in disease periods of mental and emotional imbalance of quite long standing are present before specific glandular breakdown becomes noticeable.

Calm positive mental states are an aid to health. When many planets are in watery signs in the chart, or the Moon receives afflictions of considerable strength, emotional elements tend to get the upper hand, and cause disturbances to the health.

CASE HISTORIES

(Edward Doane's writings on astrology and health solicited a huge mail from practically every State in the Union and put him in communication with doctors in various parts of the globe. In these cases he never advised the patient directly, he would give his findings to the doctor. He acted as a consultant, leaving the decision up to the doctor. He was also able to assist his students in becoming proficient in the art of stellar healing and diet.–Ed.)

Chart A is that of a daughter of one of my students. It is one of those cases where a member of the family studying astrology resulted in saving the life of another member of the family. Had it not been for stellar diagnosis being able to point out what was really the matter, this girl would have been gathered to the other side ere now.

Upon becoming ill (chart as progressed) she was taken to a doctor who utilized orthodox methods of diagnosis, and her trouble was diagnosed as tonsilitis. A blood count was made, showing anemia so far advanced that attending physicians were afraid to operate. The mother got busy with stellar diagnosis and dietetics.

If the student will consult the book by my spouse, Doris Chase Doane, entitled "Astrology: 30 Years Research," he will find that the constants for anemia are present: Neptune and Saturn prominent, usually severely afflicted. Mars also afflicted.

Sun is opposition Saturn in the natal chart. Neptune squares the Moon. Uranus semisquares Mars within two minutes of perfect. The trouble is described in detail in the Brotherhood of Light Lessons; instead of repeating it here, I'll use the space to better advantage. The Neptune squares with Venus and Moon indicate tonsilitis. Mercury, ruler of

ASTROLOGY AND EXTRASENSORY PERCEPTION

Ascendant is in the sixth house, opposing Juipter by progression. Progressed Venus is square Neptune; and Mars has progressed within orb to the conjunction of Venus.

The presence of Pluto in Cancer, plus the square of Neptune with Moon, gives this native an exceptionally sensitive stomach. The opposition of Mercury to Jupiter, plus the natal inconjunct of Mars and Saturn had mapped impacted matter collecting on the intestinal tract. This was removed by a series of colonic irrigations. You will note that Saturn in Virgo is stronger as mapping an affliction to this area than Jupiter maps its protection.

Depletion of the ability of the kidneys to eliminate toxins is signified by the afflicted Venus and natal Mars. This poison had collected in the system in large quantities; and in connection with absorption through the intestinal ferment, had caused the poisons to literally back up until the tonsils became affected.

Please note that while tonsils can become infected for various reasons, they are usually an excellent barometer indicating the presence of accumulated poisons in other parts of the organism.

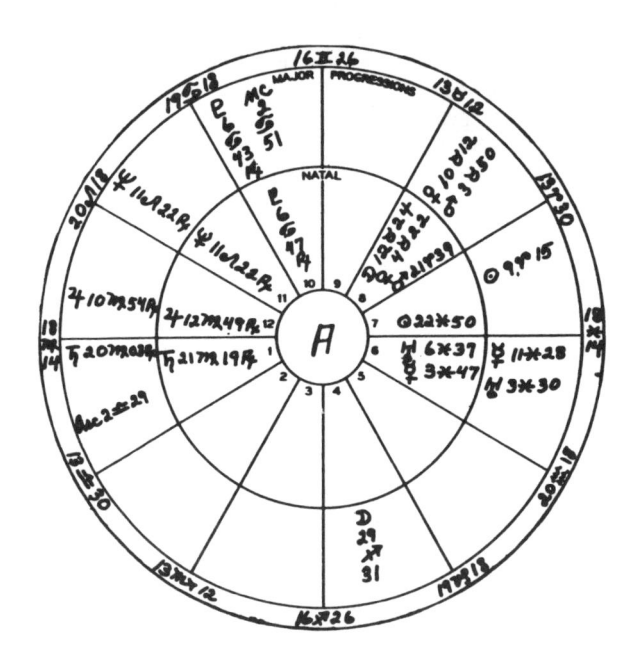

Unwise diet, including consumption of sugars and starches, in candies, drinks, white bread, potatoes, etc., had brought about a severe case of acidosis. This in connection with the other two sources of poison results in much bloating and would have soon caused death had steps not have been taken to eliminate and neutralize.

After the first colonic, this girl was placed on a liquid diet for almost a month of celery and carrot juice, including tops, some parsley juice added, and also fruit juice.

Because Venus entered in, iodine was needed (Goiter had started to become noticeable) and supplied in sea vegetation in tablet form. Vitamin E from lettuce juice was added to assist the internal secretion of the gonads. After the liquid period, wheat germ meal was added to supply more of the minerals and vitamins for which this system was literally starved. Whole wheat and soy bean bread were added and some cottage cheese. The last furnished complete proteins. Meat was eliminated entirely from the diet, for, as this chart indicates, she would never at any time in life be able to handle meat proteins successfully.

The adrenals are not strong enough. Since Jupiter was afflicted, the liver needed attention. Rhubarb laxative was used, and tomato juice (10 ounces at a time) with half a lemon squeezed in it was used three times per week on an empty stomach.

Cucumber juice (extracted seeds, peeling and all) was used to flush the kidneys more than the citrus juices alone would do.

One egg yolk beaten in fruit juice (orange or grapefruit) was added to supply sulphur for the pancreas (Jupiter). The cottage cheese (excellent where milk can not be handled successfully as in this case with Neptune square Moon) supplied, in connection with the vegetable juices and fruit juices, an abundance of calcium.

The amount of fruit juices suggested was approximately a quart daily, and entire pint of the vegetable juices, with cucumber and lettuce as extras.

A wide variety of green leaf vegetables (cooked, but not over-cooked) was added to the diet. These were cooked with olive oil and very little water.

During her illness, she had a fear of death. In her chart this is mapped by a prominent Saturn, and Neptune square the Moon in her eighth house. Stellar healing was utilized with excellent results.

Some bone marrow broth (fresh) was utilized in building back the red corpuscles in the blood stream. Pork (Saturn) that she had eaten frequently in the past was poisonous to her system. Fish (Neptune-Pisces) could not be handled so well. Rich foods (afflicted natal Jupiter) were bound to react when progressed conditions allowed.

As a result of adjusting her diet to her individual needs and cleansing her system, her symptoms disappeared. She looks and feels well, better than she had ever hoped to look and feel. She has become a devotee of the

Religion of the Stars, as indicated by the good Pluto trine Uranus and Mercury in her chart.

As Chart B illustrates, human relations sometimes exert quite a profound influence upon the health. And in order to correct the conditions resulting from these relations, it becomes necessary to make readjustments.

Mercury, ruling the cusp of the tenth house, signifying the mother, squaring the planets in Gemini signifies the tension that would be present in the daughter's home when the mother lived with her.

True to chart indications, this home had tension in it until arrangements were made for the mother to live elsewhere. The mother and daughter's husband, while getting along on the surface, had so much basic conflict between them that the magnetic discord was in marked evidence.

Saturn opposing Moon, Mars and Pluto and partaking of the square with Mercury indicates how the thoughts (Saturn in third) would be depressed and the physical body affected by this dicord. Over some years, the continual hammering of discordant energies and depressing thoughts had attracted the mind away from the conciliating Jupiter, which makes the natal sextile and trine to the opposing planets, and the conjunction Venus in the first house.

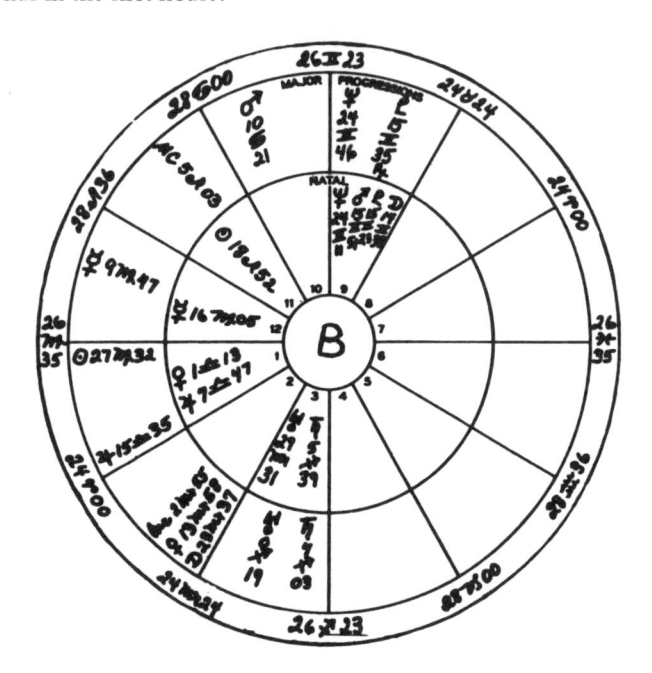

When this student's chart was erected, and the source of discord pointed out to her, suggestions made as to how to correct the dietetic deficiencies (Saturn), and how to cultivate the religious urges (faith in self) and social urges (deliberately attending movies, etc., and going to visit friends); the discord started to resolve itself into the harmonious first house outlet. While Jupiter had progressed to the trine of Mars and Pluto, the energies were not being used because of the long painful conditioning of the square. Also, progressed Mars sextiled progressed Mercury, stirring up the energies mapped by the close natal square of these two planets.

This means, that so long as the energies were being expended in one direction, they could not be expressed in some other. When the method was pointed out by which these energies could be diverted into wholly harmonious channels, and this course followed, quick changes in physical health became evident.

In our Sunday Healing Service the astral energies of the Sun, Venus and Jupiter were utilized to assist in bringing about the change. The beneficial change was a joy to behold.

The transformation was from an individual that the burdens and discords of life had come entirely too near conquering, to a happy, healthy person, who looks ahead to mental and spiritual progress with keen anticipation. Since the religious urges (Jupiter) provided the natural mental antidote for the discordant intellectual urges (Mercury), and the social urges (Venus) provided the natural mental antidote for the discordant safety urges (Saturn), and the power urges (Sun) are harmonious to the Gemini planets, the stellar healing produced such quick results as to be immediately noticeable.

This is only one of the many thousands of persons whose lives could be completely changed by a constructive utilization of the energies already present, as mapped by their charts, and assisted by stellar healing.

Some obstacles are a little too big for individuals to conquer all at once, just as some cliffs can not be scaled by attempting to go straight up the face of them. But with obstacles and cliffs there is usually a way to reach the desired objective if but one knows it. Astrology points out the pathway when there is one around the obstacle as it did in this case. When there is no pathway around, then the application of mental alchemy and stellar healing shows how to turn the obstacle into a trine or sextile and produce harmonious manifestations in the life.

Seeing a square in a chart is of no value whatsoever unless one also sees what to do in order to readjust the life so that the energies can be expended in a harmonious manner. This means that the thought elements mapped by squares are painfully conditioned relative to the departments of life involved, and to each other. Reconditioning in a pleasurable manner produces harmony, health, happiness and success.

I cannot urge too strongly that students and teachers utilize information contained in the Brotherhood of Light Lessons to bring about better states of being in their own lives and in the lives of others. To change from a condition of dis-ease to one of ease or health, whether it be physical, mental or spiritual, one must do something in a different manner than the one that has become habitual. A rut must be gotten out of, and a new trail (to the individual) broken.

This requires that some sacrifice be made. One cannot think just the same and advance mentally or think, feel and act just the same and advance spiritually, or eat and think just the same and advance physically. Motion requires constant change—capturing, storing and releasing new energies. When one makes an advance, it is a mistake to call the old state which is left behind a sacrifice. Rather it is a great privilege to be permitted to exchange disease for health, pain for pleasure, narrow vision for the Cosmic Viewpoint, mental ruts for mental progress, and material blindness for spiritual insight.

In Chart C, the birth chart constant for blood poison is a heavily afflicted Mars, and the progressed constant is an aspect to Mars with other progressed afflictions which act as rallying forces.

Natal Mars is square Jupiter and sesquisquare Pluto. At the time of his illness, Uranus had retrograded to the opposition natal Moon, and Mercury had progressed to the opposition natal Uranus and within orb of semisquare progressed Saturn. Uranus was also making the trine to Mars; and progressed Neptune was sextile progressed Mercury, mapping all of the factors essential to this type of disease.

This man was employed in a hardware store. While going about his work, he bumped his shin on a wheel barrow, breaking the skin. Infection set in and three drains were put into his leg. Amputation seemed the next step in order to save his life.

He has been a heavy meat eater, which with the afflected Mars and Saturn was of course totally wrong. Other unwise dietetic habits in company with too much meat had so filled his body with toxins that blood poison was a natural eventuality.

Upon being instructed how to use rhythmic breathing and direct the energies to the part afflicted, and instructed in the advantages of a low protein diet, his fever was reduced in 24 hours. He started on the road up.

The instruction brought about a complete change in methods of living and methods of thinking. He obtained sufficient calcium, phosphorous and Vitamin D from fruit juices, green leaf vegetables (raw) and eggs, with some milk added. The meats were eliminated completely, and orange juice substituted for somewhat stronger drinks.

You will note that the element of faith (religious urges) is indicated in his chart. After becoming convinced of the practicality of the suggestions offered him, he applied them in full measure. As a result nerve tension became conspicuous by its absence.

There was no necessity for amputation. As a matter of fact, he became one of the most calm, positive individuals it has been my pleasure to contact. He became a perservering student of the occult sciences, which he still pursues at every available moment.

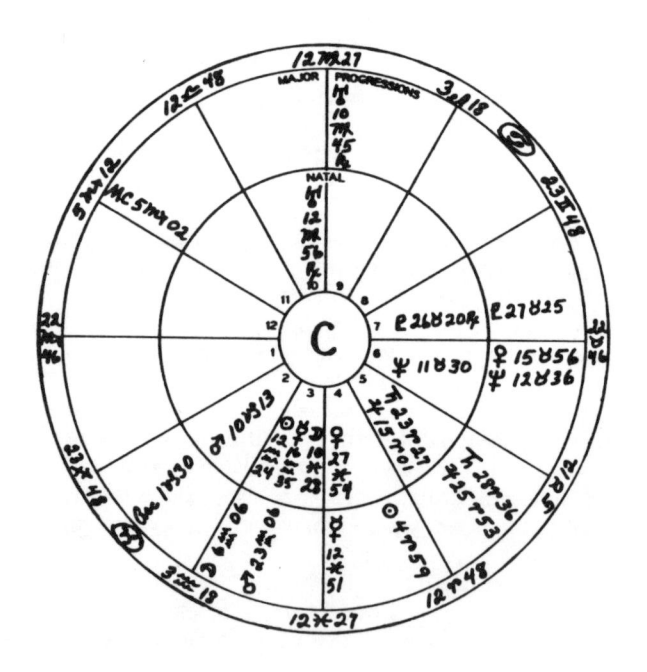

In all charts having both Saturn and Mars afflicted, meats do not come within the category of good foods for those persons. To maintain good health, it is imperative that they seek adequate proteins elsewhere. Otherwise, with the added strain on the adrenals, and the putrefactive bacteria, there is such an accumulation of toxins present that disease of some sort will break out the first time there is a progressed aspect to both the ruler of the first and sixth houses.

While dietetics can do much to assist a cure, it can do much more to prevent the necessity of a cure, if utilized in time. In other words, using indicated foods (precautions) before a disease has a chance to manifest is more effective than after the onset of the illness. This is what we call Control of Life.

The planets in a chart represent an accurate map of the condition of the glands, and indicate whether they are under functioning or over functioning, by the type of the planets entering into the affliction. In either case, the type of foods that provide the basic raw materials for the hormones is necessary to the normal function of the glands.

The soy bean provides a protein as complete as any meat, containing all essentials. It has the added advantage of being highly alkaline. A baby who won the prize for being the most healthy child in a contest had been fed soy bean cereals exclusively throughout his cereal eating life. He certainly showed the effect of careful attention to the alkaline ratio. (For those who desire his horoscope, the data: July 30, 1935, 8:47 P.M. EST, 25N50 80W15.)

One would not usually think there was any correspondence between the type of diet essential to severe burns and tuberculosis. But in both cases there is an excess of unusable proteins to be disposed of, which, unless an unusual amount of alkaline foods be taken, will poison the blood stream and increase the liability to other afflictions. Hence fruit and vegetable juices are excellent in either case, and meats, nuts and too much cereals are contra-indicated.

There is also a close correspondence between asthma and eczema, as a study of the constant factors will reveal; the exception being that in eczema, Venus enters in bringing the thyroid gland and the skin into the picture. Both depend upon undue sensitiveness of the nervous system in a given area, and both need the balance of the parathyroid glands restored, and require identical types of diet except the additional iodine for the Venus affliction in eczema.

Usually in both cases, there is an impaired eliminative function, plus insufficient calcium and vitamins in the system. Attention to the elimination, and to the mineral and vitamins, particularly in the form of vegetable juices, assist in a quick restoration to normalcy. Understandably, mental antidotes are included. In this manner the mental, physical and spiritual phases of man are treated in order to bring healthy balance into his expression.

Healing is part of our Sunday Service. The man whose chart appears here (Chart D) was attracted to us in the spring of 1938. At that time, his back had an S curve, making physical action difficult and painful. His left leg, little muscle and flesh being left on it, was afflicted with quite advanced atrophy.

His first pronounced symptoms put him to bed in 1929, when the Sun made the square to the Saturn-Pluto opposition. He had been unable to work, or indeed to get around much, since then.

Noting the constants for ear trouble, the student will see that they are Saturn and Moon, prominent and afflicted. In this case the Moon opposes Uranus and Saturn opposes Pluto. He had had a discharge from the ears since birth.

He was instructed in dietetics; the deficiencies being pointed out to him, which he corrected, largely through vegetable and fruit juices, and wheat germ meal, so that the missing mineral elements would be available to his system to help it rebuild.

Then through attending our services, Stellar Healing was applied, and almost immediate improvement set in. His spine became as straight as anyone's; his left leg is as good as the right; and his hearing and ear condition improved.

Because of the Saturn affliction, he was the victim of mineral-poor acidosis, and actual nerve starvation. The spleen was very leaky (Saturn and negative states), and he had about given up hope. In the stellar treatment, the Venus and Sun astral energies were applied directly to the hip and sciatic nerve (Sagittarius). The spleen was recharged (many times) and the structure literally rebuilt, and the energy sealed in each time as indicated in Zain's Stellar Healing. The entire spinal column was revitalized with Solar etheric and astral energies and visualized as straight.

The atrophied leg was also given Mars astral energies, and muscular activity engendered in it by direct command, so that circulation could be restored. In this phase, each muscle in the leg would work just as though a group of physical masseurs, each with a single muscle, were working all at once.

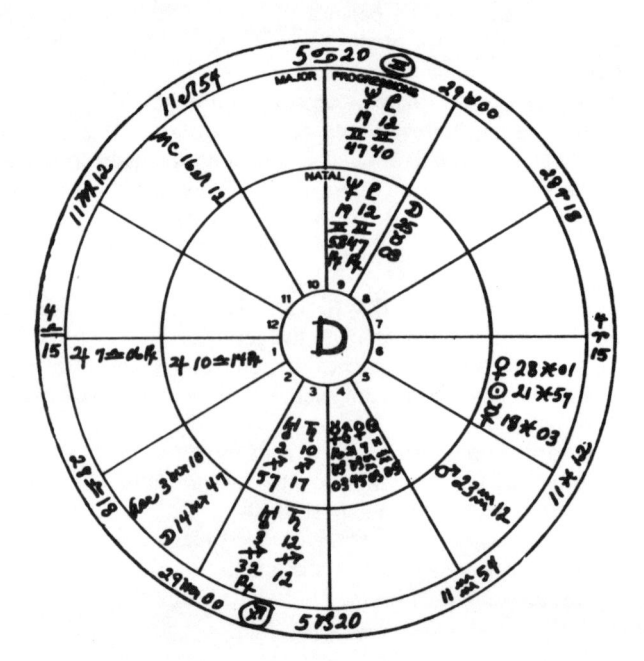

Then, because of the intense pain, a ray, which I call sedative, because I know no other name for it, was used to stop the pain with great effectiveness.

Because of his conciliating Jupiter in the first house, which is also trine Sun, every effort was made to get him to cultivate faith in himself and in higher powers; which brought into being the good health angle of Jupiter trine Sun and took advantage of the energies mapped by the sextile to Saturn and trine to Pluto.

The cerebellum was charged with Lunar etheric energies to assist in counteracting the natal opposition Uranus.

Naturally, so long as Saturnine (discordant safety urges) thoughts dominated the mind and discouragement was present, the opposition would be in full effect. But with the religious urges cultivated as the chief thought family, instead of the opposition manifesting, the sextile and trine would be brought into use.

Later this man gave talks at health food restaurants on heavenly healing powers. His desire was to tell others of his own experience and to heal. His face literally shone with a new light, and he will go forth in the world and do likewise.

This case is brought up not to attempt to exalt anyone's egoistic sense, but to illustrate that so long as life persists, there is hope. In utilizing corrective dietetics and stellar healing, much can be done for apparently hopeless cases, even though orthodox methods have failed.

Like this man, many people have neglected to use their potentialities as indicated in their natal charts. His and other cases are proof positive of the enormous value of astrology. This potential of astrology more than offsets the occasional destructive use of it.

It is my belief that someone in each occult study center should study stellar healing with a view to making it a part of regular services. It is, I assure you, a glorious privilege to be enabled to thus help others.

Then, too, practice in psychic diagnosis is an excellent phase of the work to cultivate. It is possible to visualize each part of the body and to see just what condition that part is in.

In this particular case, the skeletal structure was taken as one unit and examined thoroughly. X-ray films, which had been taken before the examination, verified this part of the findings. Then the brain and nervous system were taken as another unit, and congested nerve areas found. Then the blood vessels were taken as another unit.

This is pointed out to let the student know that there are many phases of the work that are valuable and can be cultivated to a high degree of accuracy.

Another phase of stellar healing is where one consciously cooperates with the inner-plane Brothers of Light. The brothers select the particular needed rays, and the healer serves as a tuning and transmitting agent of these high tension energies.

In no case of positive healing is it necessary to take on the condition of the patient, even though it may be felt for a little time, without danger.

My own experience indicates to me that the healer should feel rejuvenated through absorbing some of the healing energies as they pass through his body.

Students can specialize nicely, after gaining a working knowledge of all of the Brotherhood of Light Lessons. In the healing field, there is an unlimited potential for expanding this phase of the work. And it is Good Work, enabling one to relieve much physical and mental suffering, thus fulfilling his mission on earth.

EXPERIENCES

THE BEST course of thought, feeling and action is that which contributes most to Universal Welfare. Brought down to earth, it is that which does the most good for the most people.

Almost 34 years ago I was conducting the affairs of The Church of Light in Miami. A man on crutches came to one of our Sunday services. After our healing service and the close of the meeting, he stated that he could feel an energy.

The next day he returned and asked me to help him. Questioning brought out the fact that he had suffered spinal meningitis and that his spine had grown together on one side. I told him, "We will do what we can."

Using the methods of stellar healing, in which specific energies of the planets are tuned in on and directed, we were instrumental in enabling him to discard his crutches, and stand erect with a completely normal spine. It was called a miracle by those who knew of it.

The energies we used at that time are always present in full volume. The problem is to use induced emotion and directed thinking in tuning in on these energies and using them constructively. Unless they are used constructively, it is possible to add to the already present discord, for uncontrolled emotions hinder instead of assist the demonstration.

These energies are the property of The Creator we call God. Without them, we could do nothing. With them, we have unlimited possibilities for Soul Progression and contributing to Universal Welfare.

There is more to the story. After the healing had occurred and during the healed man's attendance at Sunday services, the United States became engaged in World War II. I had observed the attempts of this man to spread anti-Semitism in the manner of Hitler. Since his healing, I had noticed that he made no effort to obtain a job and earn money. A few questions brought out the story that he was supposed to be getting living expenses from his wife who was working as a domestic in New York.

Soon after the United States entered the war, he left Miami and went to a resort in Virginia. I received a letter from him. Thinking the whole matter over and remembering that he was of German birth, I decided that his wife could not possibly earn sufficient funds as a domestic to support him at a resort and that there were many contradictions in the stories he had told. I suspected that he was a possible enemy agent and reported the matter to the FBI. As a result he was picked up and held as an undesirable alien for the duration.

In this matter, it was necessary to talk with representatives from the U.S. Department of Justice, the Federal Bureau of Investigation and the Immigration Service. It was one of the latter who seemed surprised that we would be instrumental in healing this man and then reporting him to the authorities. We replied that with the many submarines just off the Florida coast line, it would be possible for him to place **many lives** in peril and that in our opinion we were doing our duty as a citizen of the United States.

All of which is to say that we believed we were assisting in the greatest good to the most people by being the instrument through which this man was detained for the duration, even though we had been the instrument through which he had been healed.

At that time the forces represented by Hitler and Company were trying to deprive the entire world of all freedom. Today the forces of Atheistic Materialism, as represented by the Communism of U.S.S.R. and Red China, are trying the same thing by force of arms and by subversion. These, too, are direct representatives of those inner plane forces we call the Inversive Brotherhood.

These are aided and abetted by all those who advocate a materialistic philosophy no matter what they pretend to be. It should also be noted that those of the extreme right, who advocate turning back the evolutionary clock or believe in violence and suppression, are assisting (without being aware of it) in creating the conditions which allow the subversion of the left to be most effective. They too are tools of the same Inversive Brotherhood on the inner planes.

The best possible course of action for a person or a nation that believes in freedom usually lies somewhere between advocated extremes. And be it noted that we of The Church of Light have not hesitated and will not hesitate to report to the proper governmental authorities those we believe are working (mentally as well as physically) for the enslavement of the human race, even though such persons might be members of our Church, or though we might have been the instruments through which they received healing or other benefits. We believe such action is in the interest of Universal Welfare and that the cause of freedom must not only be preserved but must be advanced as rapidly as possible.

During 1934 it became necessary for me to write to Elbert Benjamine, founder of the Church of Light in Los Angeles, telling him of the plans of an individual who had applied for a Church charter to place a negative person (with no knowledge of The Religion of The Stars) in the pulpit to conduct services and to use the Church as a front for commercial operations in astrology. This person had written of his plans to J.J. Hall in Tampa, Florida, who promptly sent the letter to me. Suffice it to say that the plans were blocked.

During the same time I was conducting rather intensive research in various forms of Extrasensory Perception. One evening while working with clairvoyance, I saw a pair of eyes approaching me. These eyes came up quite close and I knew that not a shred of my character was hidden from them. They seemed completely impartial. Some few years later when a picture of Elbert Benjamine was published, I recognized the eyes as belonging to him and wrote and told him of the incident.

Such was the modesty of the man that only once during our many years of close association did he refer to it, and then (when asking me to come to Los Angeles to assist him), he wrote, "Knowing more about you than most people realize."

With his many talents and very highly developed extrasensory abilities, he had no use for pretense and sham. Since he was using the powers of his mind on the astral plane and since I was tuned in on that level when I saw his eyes, this experience brought home to me in an unforgettable manner one of the truths of our religion. It is this: on the inner planes, the character stands revealed for all to see. Thus those who try to create a false image of themselves in the hope of deceiving others deceive themselves most of all. The proper way to win respect and admiration is to build the kind of character and indulge in the types of thought, feeling and action that are admirable and which in the long run contribute most to universal welfare.

C. C. Zain (Elbert Benjamine) was selected to write The Brotherhood of Light Lessons and to re-establish The Religion of The Stars on earth because (so far as I have been able to ascertain) he was the only person on earth possessing the necessary talents, the right sort of character and the driving desire to contribute his utmost to universal welfare. That he completed his earthly task most admirably is attested to by the Brotherhood of Light Lessons themselves.

A tax assessor once asked me, "What does he get out of it?" My answer was, "Not a thing except the soul satisfaction of knowing he has done his best for humanity." and so he did, leaving us a priceless heritage and the teachings which will enable humankind to build a new and better civilization here on earth in this Aquarian Age.

Back in 1943 just after I had moved to Los Angeles at the request of Elbert Benjamine, I met a young man who had become a member of the Church. We used to take occasional walks on Sunday afternoons. Almost every time we met, he would ask me about some problem and try to get me to tell him what to do. Instead I would, to the best of my ability, analyze the problem and try to get him to see the various aspects of it. On occasion he would lose control of his emotions and become a bit angry because I would never tell him what to do. Some five years later he thanked me for not trying to do his thinking for him, for he had finally realized that I was doing him a favor in forcing him to make his own decisions.

For an individual soul to make much progress, it must learn to accept full responsibility for its own thoughts, feelings, and actions. It must learn that its own attitudes toward people, events and circumstances determine whether or not it is advancing toward a more spiritual state of being or slipping backward toward a brute level of consciousness.

As one embraces more and more of the teachings of The Religion of The Stars and works away at the twin problems of making individual Soul Progression and assisting the Divine Plan of Progressive Evolution, the entire character undergoes beneficial changes. Gradually discord is replaced by harmony as a result of changed and changing attitudes brought about by greater understanding and increasing desire to work with God and the Legions of Light in the great task ahead in this New Age.

To an unevolved soul, a person who (in the opinion of the unevolved one) has done something less than admirable in the eyes of society becomes subject to condemnation. The unevolved soul does not realize that he takes such an attitude because the person he condemns acted on his own without consulting the unevolved one about it. In short, the unevolved would be happy (so he thinks) if he could just control the thoughts, utterances and acts of the other person.

To a soul a bit higher up the ladder of initiation, the person some would condemn is a necessary part of the Divine Plan; and while he might be in error upon occasion (as we all are), he is none the less gaining experience which will allow for soul progression. Rather than condemning him, we offer every encouragement to assist him in being a truly independent entity working out his own salvation.

We never try to do anyone's thinking for him. All our efforts and all of the teachings of the Religion of The Stars are directed toward enabling the individual to become a truly free soul, to climb the initiatory ladder of Soul Progression, and to learn to work consciously with the Legions of Light and Eternal God in realizing the Divine Plan here on earth.

While no one else I have ever known, including self, has developed his extrasensory perception to as high a degree as C. C. Zain, each of us has potentials that can be developed and used in our efforts to advance our own souls and to assist God.

And while on occasion our efforts may be misunderstood and resented by those whose attitudes are not the best, or whose motives the highest, we can remember the age-old admonition: Expect ye not gratitude from men. We can receive soul satisfaction from the fact that we are doing our best for evolving humanity and assisting our own souls to make progress at the same time.

We ask for your continued assistance that we may bring the Message of the Aquarian Age to as many as is possible. Working together in harmonious cooperation with the Legions of Light who are servants of Eternal God, free souls can and will build the New Civilization here on earth.

AQUARIAN AGE GUIDANCE

KNOW Yourself, and Give Yourself. This is one of the occult admonitions that should be repeated and taken into meditation frequently.

In the past 50 years since we personally contacted the teachings of the Religion of the Stars on earth, we have known many who have studied the lessons to some degree. We have also known many who became members of the Church of Light, and, who through answering the final examination questions furnished with each Course, became Hermeticians. Of these, there were a few who studied and restudied in order to find the means of climbing the ladder of soul initiation toward Adeptship.

The first requisite to Knowing Yourself is a completely sincere desire to ascertain the facts so that you might eliminate those habit-systems of thought, feeling and action which in the past have been followed by painful consequences to yourself and others.

This requires the determination to be completely honest with yourself. It also requires that you study to gain the ability to analyze and discriminate. The Brotherhood of Light Lessons afford the essential information which includes astrology, esoteric psychology, and the alchemies—personal, mental, spiritual and cosmic.

Astrology is essential, because it provides the only map of elements of the subconscious mind or soul, as it existed at the moment of birth into human form. Esoteric psychology and the alchemies are essential because these provide the means of understanding mental processes and the proper manner of transmuting the elements of the animal soul into the elements of the divine soul.

After you have gained the essential information through study, assuming that your desire to know is sufficiently strong, you are ready to sit down with your natal chart, your memory, and your God to get acquainted with the hitherto unknown you.

You proceed to use your memory, going back over the events and circumstances of your life in relation to your chart to determine the progressions under which these occurred and your attitudes and reactions to these events and circumstances.

Using the positive and negative keywords associated with each sign and planet (including the Sun and the Moon), you determine to some degree how you have reacted (thought, felt and acted) in each case and how you should have reacted.

From personal experience, we know that you will not be proud of the emotional childishness your analysis reveals. But we also know that should you desire to Be Yourself, you will realize that you have to face the facts of yourself as you are at this point. Then firmly resolve to begin the lifelong task of climbing the ladder toward an ever increasing spirituality with true Adeptship at the top of the climb.

You will realize that each soul is an independent entity, working out its own salvation as a minute but essential part of the Divine Plan. You will understand now why astrology is called the Golden Key. It has enabled you to Know Yourself, Be Yourself, and to prepare to join God in the fulfillment of the Divine Plan through Giving Yourself.

You will also learn that you must cultivate patience with yourself. One way to do this is to realize that you have an eternity of spiritual progress ahead of you.

Permit a personal observation here. During the course of our own studies of The Brotherhood of Light Lessons (we still study them), we realized that for over 20 years members of our inner-plane organization had been watching over us—impressing us to take moves which led up to our determination to devote the rest of physical existence to the Great Work.

One time when we were thinking about the great patience shown by the inner-plane Brothers through the years, we felt humble because of our own waywardness of thought and feeling. The Brothers impressed us with, "you people (meaning we earthlings) do not know anything about patience."

In musing on the eons of time necessary to evolve and direct the functions of a solar system or a universe, we quite agreed that we did not know anything about patience. Nonetheless, each progressing soul must work to build the virtue of patience into his makeup.

Among the many students who became Hermeticians, we have known those whose only purpose in study was to find the answers to the final examination questions and be entitled to put the word Hermetician after their names.

These souls never discovered the highest usage of astrology or realized any of the spiritual benefits to be obtained by obeying the admonition: Know Yourself, Be Yourself and Give Yourself. Most of them never gained any comprehension of what is contained in the Brotherhood of Light Lessons. Of course, these souls imagined they knew. But since the idea that character development is essential to spiritual progress never occurred to them, they derived no benefit from their studies.

Our Church was incorporated to teach, practice and disseminate the Religion of The Stars. In the spiritual sense, it is impossible for any soul to gain personal benefit from our religion in any other manner than through the practice of our religion.

Know Thyself keys the first step in gaining the ability to practice. In our view, the teaching and dissemination are very important to present and future generations. Yet we must not overlook an all important fact. It is the practice from which individual souls benefit. Therefore, to gain proficiency in practice is to know and understand oneself and squarely face the facts and factors of eternal life.

Developing skill in the use of Extrasensory Perception is desirable as is developing skill in analyzing birth charts through astrology. But of vastly more importance to the individual soul aspiring to ascend the ladder to Adeptship is developing skill in Directed Thinking and Induced Emotion.

Directed Thinking enables correct analysis and true discrimination. Induced Emotion enables one to effectively use the problem attitude and pleasure technique as a means of constantly improving the character and thus developing spirituality.

As stated earlier, we still study the Brotherhood of Light Lessons. We still find them a veritable gold mine of information, useful to our soul in our own efforts to climb ever higher up the ladder toward Adeptship.

We have never known anyone, including C. C. Zain with whom we worked directly for 16 years, who had the intellectual capacity to memorize and retain for instant usage all of the vast amount of information contained in the Lessons.

Even though he was the physical channel through which the Religion of The Stars was reestablished upon earth, like ourselves, he found it necessary to refer to the Lessons constantly to assist the progress of his soul in eternal life. As a result of our experiences, we have a rather comprehensive understanding of how little of the teachings entered the minds of those who studied with the sole desire of passing the final exams.

We have observed others who studied some or all of the Lessons who were searching for statements and ideas to bolster their own preconceived opinions. Many of these upon finding material that directly contradicted their opinions ceased at that point to study. This is just another way of saying that the desire to Know Yourself was completely absent in these closed minds, and that they were not yet ready for the soul-uplifting teachings of the Religion of The Stars.

Another admonition: This above all else to your own self be true, and it must follow as does the night the day, you cannot then be false to any man.

Obviously, being true to one's self demands getting acquainted with that same self. Yet many who imagine they are seeking truth overlook this fact. The idea of using a knowledge of astrology to analyze one's own habit-systems of thought, feeling and action to gain an understanding of one's own soul has not occurred to them. Yet this is the highest personal application of astrology. As a consequence, a most important step in being true to one's self is overlooked.

In order to know one's self and to be true to one's self, all opinions of self-importance must be set aside. It is necessary to understand that whatever attainments one may have on earth, one's mind is still as the mind of a little child when compared to the minds of those exalted souls from whom the teachings of our religion emanated.

Many years ago we found it necessary to conduct a study of astronomy. With the assistance of physical textbooks and our spiritual tutors, we were working away at the problem of trying to gain a clear picture of the various motions of the earth. Thus we were directly tuned in on the minds of our inner-plane tutors. At one point we heard them laughing at our mental efforts to comprehend the factors involved. But it was kindly laughter. We could understand that our mental struggles appeared to them as the mental struggles of a two-year-old infant would appear to us. We also realized that we were being helped because in the view of those exalted souls, we too had work to do in assisting the Divine Plan of Progressive Evolution.

Uncritical mysticism, the blind acceptance of statements upon authority, is the greatest foe to human progress. This is because such practice bars the development of skill in directed thinking and keeps out of the mind the possibility of using the searchlight of critical analysis.

Recently we received a letter in which the individual pretended to be a superior mind and referred to other minds as inferior. The person also recited a long list of authors as the basis of what he termed "Truth." Since some of the authorities cited were self contradictory, we doubted the claim to superiority. A comment from the inner planes on the letter, "The boy puts himself on quite a pedestal, doesn't he?"

Another saying that comes to us directly from the same source as the Brotherhood of Light Lessons is, "A wise person is ever mindful of how little he knows, while a fool is ever prideful of how much he knows."

Because the mind of any embodied human being is as the mind of a little child relative to those exalted minds on the spiritual levels of the inner plane, boasting is ever a sign of ignorance. To any individual, knowledge is that which he is able to prove for himself.

Critical Analysis must always precede intelligent comparison and the determination to gain truth for self. Failure to recognize and develop this potential which is latent in every soul, keeps the mind vulnerable to all sorts of false assumptions and ideas in religious and scientific fields. So long as an individual soul blindly accepts, the progress of that soul is limited.

No matter from whom or where it may emanate, the written or spoken word is merely information. The accuracy or inaccuracy of the information can be determined by the individual only when the ability is developed to use the searchlight of critical analysis. In case of a religious practice, including the practice of the Religion of The Stars, this can be determined only as the information is tested in the laboratory of life.

We have never found anyone who would disagree with the statement: "Every person must think and feel for self. It is impossible for any person to think and feel for anyone else."

We have never found anyone who would disagree with the statement: "No matter with which religious organization one is affiliated, there is just one possession a person can take with him through the gateway of death. That is the character he builds for himself while in the flesh."

In our view, the above statements are self-evident truths. To build character in the most efficient manner requires an analysis of the habit-systems of thinking, feeling and action. That is, one must obey the ancient admonition: Know Yourself.

Since it is impossible for any person to be any other person than self, it is necessary that you learn to Be Yourself. To claim one's Divine Heritage as a minute but essential part of the Divine Plan, it is necessary to learn to Give Yourself in unselfish service in assisting the progress of that Divine Plan.

But it is each individual soul that is an independent entity working out its own salvation that must provide the right sort of energy to stir the soul to become a true neophyte and accept its own self-evident responsibilities.

The person who only pretends to be desirous of becoming spiritual can always find ways to rationalize and distort the facts of eternal life. Some of these we have known use their own birth charts as a scapegoat. They say, "I can't do that because of such-and-such afflictions in my chart."

Others try to flee reality by blaming other people, saying, he or she (and sometimes it) makes me happy, glad, mad and a multitude of other things totally impossible. Each person must think, feel and act for self. No other person· or condition makes a person· "anything," including the personal birth chart. It is the thinking, feeling and acting of each one that makes "everything" about that one.

Therefore, trying to escape one's responsibility for one's own soul, for building one's own character, and thus determining one's own destiny—when physical existence comes to an end—is to be foolish.

Every person possesses the potentiality of unlimited expansion of consciousness and of soul progression far beyond the ability of most people to understand in their present state of development. Yet every person must become aware of self and the Divine Potentials of that self before much progress can be made. It is for this reason that the admonition of Know Yourself, Be Yourself, and Give Yourself, is of such vast importance.

To be successful in the practice of the Religion of The Stars requires that one obey the above admonition and thus bring about the gradual changes in character that raise the basic character vibratory rate of the soul to continually higher levels as the spirituality increases.

In this practice, one learns to build within one's own soul the peace and understanding that comes as a natural consequence of working with God. He also strives for self-improvement in order to become a better servant of God and to be better able to assist struggling souls to find and travel the same pathway.

We do not view the various minds (souls) as either inferior or superior. Rather, we view each one as we view ourselves—a minute but necessary part of the Divine Whole undergoing experiences which will ultimately (here or hereafter) enable them to obey the ancient admonition: Know Yourself, Be Yourself, and Give Yourself. Then they enter into free will cooperation with God and His Plan.

Therefore, those born under any one of the 12 signs of the zodiac are no better or worse than those born under another sign. For in each chart are all of the signs and all of the planets, which portray the individual differences of the soul at the moment of physical birth. Since we view each soul as an independent entity working out its own salvation and each soul as an essential part of God's Plan, we strive to understand, to assist when and where we can, and to help the best we may the progress of individual souls.

We view some souls as being delinquent, but not one, regardless of race, color or creed, as any more necessary or any less necessary to the Creator of all souls. Therefore, we find no particular difficulty in loving God and all of the creation of God.

To us, condemning part of Creation, or trying to sit in final judgment on some individual soul, is to state to God, "See! You have made mistakes." We are then telling Him how He should conduct Creation. To us, this is not only foolish it is extreme arrogance.

None of us are so highly evolved that we can state with certainty for just what ultimate purpose a particular soul was created to assist God in accomplishing. In short, we should learn and practice another of the admonitions of the Religion of The Stars, which is, "Think and do unto others as you would have others think and do unto you."

We have observed through the many years we have studied people and their habit-systems of thought, feeling and action that most of them mistake an emotional response for an intellectual process. That is, they leap to conclusions about some situation, process, or set of data and imagine they have thought about the matter. The assumptions accepted—whether in some field of science, religion, politics or sociology—usually contain a large measure of error.

Those who employ directed thinking and induced emotion in examining the same situations or set of data are usually correct in the final conclusion to a much larger degree.

In analyzing himself and his potentials through astrology, extrasensory perception, directed thinking and induced emotion, a person starts at the foundation to build toward the final conclusion. If he disregards the natal chart and uses what is called psychoanalysis in order to gain factual knowledge of himself, he starts, in effect, at the roof to try to discover the secrets of his subconscious mind or soul.

It has always seemed more scientific to us to begin all structures at the foundation, be they physical houses or a structure of factual information of the mental makeup and emotional elements in an individual mind. In this manner one is able to avoid much false assumption through leaping to unwarranted conclusions.

We have met many, in and out of our faith, who seem to have a sincere desire to help others. Of these many, only a few realized that even in an effort to assist another, it is possible to contribute directly to the delinquency of a soul.

For instance, if in trying to help, we use astrology which results in removing an individual's incentive to study and learn to analyze and understand for himself, we have hindered his progress.

Gaining understanding of one's own soul and the souls of others is, of necessity, a gradual and continuing process. This is because we are dealing with life in all of its multitude of relationships. In addition, we are dealing with a variety of substances and energies, embracing those of physical, astral and spiritual planes. For we need to understand the how and why to gain a more comprehensive understanding.

Thus, we must ever strive, through meditation (thinking), to enlarge our intellectual horizon to enable us to get a clearer mental picture of the problems we face as we climb toward Adeptship and find better ways of solving these problems.

Our struggle to gain understanding embraces the problems incident to the evolution of human society to the point that a genuine peace on earth is possible. And as we gain cosmic consciousness we must work to channel the thoughts, feelings and actions of humanity as a whole into harmonious patterns, even as we strive as individuals to learn to live the completely constructive life.

The doorway to spiritual attainment is always open to aspiring souls. The opportunity to gain love and wisdom is always present. An ever higher degree of consciousness is available to those who are willing to travel the pathway. Know Yourself, Be Yourself, and Give Yourself.

If our little Earth were placed on a four-foot map of the solar system in its correct size, a rather powerful microscope would be necessary in order to see it at all. When seven billion plus miles is reduced to a four foot scale even our Sun would be difficult to see.

That which seems so tremendous and disturbing to us—because we seldom adopt the wider cosmic viewpoint—is in relative proportion very small indeed. Even as our puny minds are small, in relative comprehension, when we perceive the vastness of understanding necessary to conceive, build and conduct the affairs of a Solar System such as our own.

When we understand that what is seen on Earth is a small but necessary part of a continually evolving Divine Plan of Eternal Progression, then what appears to be vastly disturbing is perceived as the natural result of the attitudes and actions of ignorance on the part of human beings who do not understand. It is also understood that the painful experiences of individuals, nations and races are the result of such ignorance. Yet these experiences provide the means by which progress may be made, if the lessons are seen and heeded.

Peace is not yet, because a sufficient number of people are either unready or unwilling to look for, try to understand and follow leadership of the Divine Being we call God. Peace results not from prayers of the ignorant, the threats of the egotistical or the destruction of nations.

Peace results from people finding and living The Life of The Spirit, thus obtaining true enlightenment and the realization that all life is ONE and all beings akin with each other and with God. Man can learn to be humble through understanding; great through conscious alliance with God; and become a constructive power through working with God in the fulfillment of The Divine Plan.

The New Age is birthing, the New Civilization undergoing gestation, and an evolving awareness is under way on Earth—small as it is in the Cosmos. Its people can become great in cosmic consciousness and willing cooperators with Eternal God.

In the minds of those of little faith, there is much turmoil, fear and apprehension. In the minds of those who have attained cosmic consciousness, there is peace with God and self, and peace with one's fellows insofar as those fellows will allow. The God of all Cosmos is the source, the haven and the refuge of all Life, Light and Love. We cannot seek higher guidance, greater wisdom or deeper compassion than is found in the Creative Whole which is Cosmos and all of its multitude of life forms.

When all the peoples of the Earth realize that they are One with the Divine Whole and start to live that realization, Peace on Earth and Good Will toward all of Creation will follow as a matter of course. Seek eternally for more and more light and the shadows cast by ignorance will disappear.

In conclusion, the following text from Zain's Spiritual Astrology is presented as a fruitful subject for meditation in seeking Divine Guidance in the Aquarian Age.

> There is no death! What seems so is transition:
> This life of mortal breath
> Is but a suburb of the life elysian
> Whose portal we call death.

Love and Wisdom are the Essence of Life

a non-profit organization

Dedicated to help mankind to help himself and others to achieve a happier and more harmonious life, to acquire knowledge that leads to scientific spiritual understanding in this Aquarian Age.

Each and every one of the Brotherhood of Light Courses, by C. C. Zain, will serve as a means to this achievement.

Laws of Occultism	Evolution of Life
Astrological Signatures	Evolution of Religion
Spiritual Alchemy	Mundane Astrology
Ancient Masonry	Occultism Applied To Daily Life
Esoteric Psychology	Weather Predicting
Sacred Tarot	Stellar Healing
Tarot Cards	Cosmic Alchemy
Spiritual Astrology	Imponderable Forces
Horary Astrology	Organic Alchemy
Mental Alchemy	The Next Life
Delineating the Horoscope	Personal Alchemy
Progressing the Horoscope	Index to the 210 Brotherhood of Light Lessons
Divination and Character Reading	Egyption Tarot Cards

These and other materials on the hermetic sciences are available from:

FOUNDATION OF SCIENTIFIC SPIRITUAL UNDERSTANDING

FOSSU

P. O. Box 93 • Redondo Beach, California 90277